BETWEEN FEAR AND FORTUNE

THE TRUTH ABOUT NETWORK MARKETING AND LIVING LIFE ON YOUR OWN TERMS

BETWEEN FEAR AND FORTUNE

JOHN HOLOWATY

To request permissions, contact the publisher at info@johnholowatymentor.com.

Paperback ISBN: 978-1-5272-7994-0

First paperback edition March 2022.

Edited by Candi Cross, You Talk, I Write
Produced by Weller Smith Design, LLC
Cover and Interior Design and Layout by LeAnna Weller Smith and Sheryl Kober for Weller Smith Design

For More Information:
www.johnholowatymentor.com

DEDICATION

This book is dedicated to anyone who still has a drive and ambition to create a dream life for themselves and their family. It's also for the amazing people that I've had the pleasure of working with during my career. I hope *Between Fear and Fortune* helps and inspires you to go further in your network marketing business and achieve your dreams as you inspire someone else to do the same, too.

CONTENTS

"If you are distressed by anything external, the pain is not due to the thing itself, but to your estimate of it; and this **you have the power** to revoke at any moment."

—MARCUS AURELIUS

INTRODUCTION

FEAR IS A FARCE

Have you ever stopped to think about what fear is? What is it made of? You know that it can be paralyzing or lead you down a long road of procrastination as it creeps up through your nervous system. But how does fear start?

I'm most drawn to Darrin Donnelly's definition of fear in his book, *Victory Favors the Fearless*. As a preface, Donnelly created his library of information, Sports for the Soul, to showcase reliable and trustworthy self-improvement advice that "actually works": life advice from the greatest minds in sports. I agree with his thinking that the sports arena has a way of cutting through fake, fluffy advice. The achiever in sports can't exaggerate his or her results. It's worth pointing out that the field of sports psychology is referred to as "the science of success" because the individual's thoughts and actions can be directly evaluated, tested, and confirmed based on their results. I may listen to a boatload of self-development masters, but when it comes to my daily actions, I also look to fitness and sports examples for greatness.

Back to fear, Donnelly writes: "Everything you do follows your mental outlook. 'This is how you become what you think about,' as psychologists say. And that is why it's so important to protect your mindset and proactively take control of your thoughts.

"Fearful thinking is one of the most damaging and destructive thought patterns you can fall into. Fears are usually repetitive—you tend to ruminate about them over and over again. Fears are also intense—they can weigh you down and make it hard to think about anything else. This combination of frequency and intensity is why fear is such a damaging emotion. Your fears hold you back from living the life you were born to live. If you're ever going to achieve success, happiness, and peace of mind, you must first defeat your fears."

Let the meaning and gravity of that message sit with you for a spell. Do you realize how much fear can control your life? You have a LIFE to live; you don't have a *fear* to live every day!

Bottom line: Even if your skills are not that of an athlete, and you prefer Broadway shows—starring in, if you're so fortunate, or viewing them—to baseball, basketball, and boxing, take on the mental outlook of an athlete. There are many reasons for this, ranging from focus and physical conditioning, discipline, mental toughness, camaraderie, and competitiveness, to fierce discipline, which I will argue is the most common attribute/act that people struggle with. Friends, the struggle is *real.* I see it all the time as a fitness trainer and mentor in the network marketing world. That's exactly why you will see story notes about triumphant athletes. Please do not just skirt over these snippets—remember they are real people, who often hurdled over rather extreme odds before winning. They weren't just pushing past a hangover, passing over a party or family celebration, or needing to lose a few pounds to fit back into the perfect black dress. And here, I don't minimize anyone's odds or struggles. The beauty of this life is individuality and being able to wave at someone on their journey from the nearby place of your journey or holding hands on a shared journey.

I see fear all the time in network marketing. "I'm skeptical," usually means "I'm scared or fearful". Fearful this may not work out or I may not be good at it. People create stories in their mind based on past experiences or based on someone else's experience.

THE FEAR OF GETTING STARTED

Let's face it: We have all signed up to something we never used, or we didn't complete. A book we bought, a course we paid for, a gym membership or a piece of fitness equipment we bought that now works as a clothes hanger or a door stop.

People can sometimes be scared of getting started because this could be another time in their life that they fail or wasted their money on something they never used. I always say that people aren't actually skeptical about your product or your business; they are skeptical about themselves. They usually ask two questions: Is the reward big enough? Can I do it? We have tons of evidence of success because we have amassed hundreds of positive stories both from the product and the business opportunity. But they don't! They only have their past experiences to compare it to.

In comes the next part of the fear and skeptical cocktail. Other people's negative opinions. Their partner talks them out of it due to their own past failures and let-downs. A friend of a friend has tried it and it didn't work for them. (The truth is *they* didn't work for it.) But you're not around to get into that debate. Now you can spend your time and energy worrying about it. Try to intervene and step in. Maybe use the "I know how you feel, I felt the same, but then I realized this!" talking points. That does work from time to time and I would never suggest taking the first no as final. However, what you have to remember is so much of this chit chat is out of your control and honestly not worth giving your energy to. The chit chat and skepticism are not action. If you are easily swayed by opinions, you're probably not a good fit for this opportunity. The less time you spend in this chit chat, the more time you have to find the right person who dives in and takes action from the word "go". Just like I did. And of course, I did my research. I read some negatives for sure. But ultimately, I was bold enough to realize that fear has killed more dreams than trying ever will, and if you want to talk about failing, you're listening to the right person.

I failed the first year of university three times in a row! Not because it was hard, but because it came down to sheer lack effort and commitment. When it came to classes, I couldn't be bothered, and when it came to revising work, I didn't want to. It wasn't my tutor's fault or the university's. I needed to take sole responsibility. I had a history of failing and stop-start job stories.

My story goes back to the two key questions: Is the reward big enough? Can I do it? Most of the things we quit at or fail in in life centers on the reward not being big enough or the pain not strong enough. I was always told I was lazy and never worked hard enough. That wasn't necessarily true. Looking back, I was bored, unmotivated and had zero interest in doing something I saw no reward in.

The lessons at school I messed around in the most, I saw as the most pointless. "I'm never going to use this stuff, so why teach it to me?" If they would have taught entrepreneurship and personal development at school, I would have shown up as two Johns!

When I became a fitness professional and found my passion, I was the hardest working trainer in the gym. To this day, I'm the hardest working leader on my team. I'm not saying my leaders don't work as hard as me, but I will never let them out-work me. They can work as hard as me but never harder. The great thing about the stories we tell ourselves is this. We can erase them and create new ones. Just like I did. If you had told the students or teachers that I went to college with that I would go on to build a global business, buy holiday homes around the world, speak on big stages and write a book as a thought leader in my industry, they would have laughed.

I have made mistakes, failed, been written off. Welcome to the club! But the great thing is we can prove them all wrong together. So, let's get to it, my friend!

FIRST BRUSH WITH REJECTION

I am anxious to answer a common question I've received over the years. In fact, this book is one big answer. What separates successful network marketers from those who give up in their first month?

They didn't get a sign-up after speaking to ten people or nobody wanted to order after a couple of social media posts. Their candle burned out quickly.

First of all, human beings have a quitter's mindset. We quit the gym,

jobs, relationships. Quitting is ingrained in a lot of people. When people join the network marketing industry, they either think it will be easy and fast or that the dream lifestyle they see on social media happens overnight. But they were supposed to get a lot of doors closed in their faces initially. Not everyone sees what you see. When they realize that people are skeptical, they give up after the first couple of "no's."

The first person that I brought into this business quit after two weeks. He thought it was going to be simple. Having that long-term vision is key. Finding what they love about it more than money is so important—the cultural element, making new friends, personal development. Diving in for that stuff more than the money helps to plant you there. Entering any profession and making big money out of the gate is rare, or a fantasy at best, without some longevity and dedication. Respecting your vision as a business requires you to see that there will be ups and downs. Improvement is a mindset. Understanding the compound effect and that this is effort related greatly increases your chances for success. The harder you work and the more people you speak to, the bigger your business will be.

There are two basic things about network marketing, any enterprising venture, or a plan B that I want you to know upfront.

First, not everyone has a "yes" and a hug for you. In fact, be prepared to receive 100 no's and frowns to go with them before earning one "YES." Every "yes" is so powerful, so exhilarating, that I promise, it will instill more confidence and push you to work harder. The sting of "no's" does become increasingly less impactful and eventually to the point that rejection is really okay as your rhino skin becomes thicker. I call it the "NO" muscle, as just like working out, when you lift weights you tear muscle fibers and it gets sore. But in three days' time, your muscle gets stronger and you can do more becoming more resistant to pain.

Fulfilling routines and taking action are progress, period. Also, check off the box of "learning experience". Plus, check off the box of "growth." This is self-development, my friend! You'll hear testimonies with these running themes and commonalities in the Success Tribe section.

Secondly, we all work in a global village. What does this mean? People connect, collaborate, and consume around the clock by a little, square device in the palm of their hands. People pivot together. People thrive together. You no longer need a dizzying amount of local, long, drawn out meetings in person to accomplish great feats, help others, make money, and live a satisfying life. And this tiny concept of diversity and inclusion (D & I) many of us operate from nowadays? A global village offers a smorgasbord of cultures, personalities, skills, strengths, and resources to draw from. You're never alone or without answers. You're never without ideas, connection, and community.

Stay close to the fire! That's where the warmth is, it's where the light is and its where the energy is.

FEAR IS A GIFT—A BIG CLAIM BUT WORTH EXAMINING

Straight away, I am going to credit Gavin de Becker, who wrote *The Gift of Fear*, for what I am about to impart here. His book opened many eyes to a new mindset around fear. At least enough to make it a No. 1 national bestseller on *The New York Times* bestseller list for seventeen weeks. After twenty years, the book remains the world's biggest-selling book on preventing violence, now published in nineteen languages. De Becker's firm has protected several thousand clients, including more than ninety of the world's most prominent families and at-risk individuals. Clearly, his business is related to safety! And mine is quite softer, with little physical danger. But wow, how fear can creep in so much that it in and of itself becomes a physical danger.

When linked to network marketing, so many people have a fear of other people's thoughts and opinions, which

RULE NO. 1:

The very fact that you fear something is solid evidence that it is not happening.

It is that which might come next that we fear—what might happen, not what is happening. He uses the example of standing near the edge of a cliff and fearing getting too close; then if you stand right at the edge, you no longer fear getting too close, you now fear falling. He goes on to point out that panic, which is the great enemy of survival, is perceived as completely unmanageable.

you have zero control over. People are so scared of what their friends will think or say about a social media post that they never end up posting or make a half-hearted attempt to share what they are doing. "I don't want to sell to my friends," they tell me. Well, for a start, you're looking at this the wrong way.

RULE NO. 2:

What you fear is rarely what you think you fear—it is what you *link* to fear.

When we get a fear signal, our intuition has already made many connections. Yep, it happens that quickly! De Becker adds: "Those who fear public speaking actually fear the loss of identity that attaches to performing badly, and that is firmly rooted in our survival needs. For all social animals, from ants to antelopes, identity is the pass card to inclusion, and inclusion is key to survival." Brilliantly put, since so many of us spend more time on stages than we may have ever wanted or planned.

If you opened a wine bar, would you invite your friends to come and check it out? Yes! Would you expect them to come down and support your business? Yes! So, if you let them know you're launching an online business, would you expect them to support you? Yes! But if you don't let them know how can they help you? Don't be apologetic for chasing your dreams. Don't be apologetic for recommending a product you believe in. Don't be apologetic for promoting your businesses. I bet the last time you checked, your friends weren't paying your bills or saving up to take your kids on holiday. And remember this: If your friends don't support your business, then you need to question if they are really friends. I'm not saying they need to buy but if they get negative, critical or are unsupportive, seriously question if you want them in your life.

You can quote me on this one: "If they aren't living the life you want to live, their opinion is invalid!"

MAKING A FORTUNE

My first encounter with the term, *fortune*, was hearing Jim Rohn's quote: "Profits are better than wages. A wage will make you a living, but a profit will make you a fortune."

I hear a lot of enthusiastic plans "to make a fortune" and I have a strong definition of fortune in my own life and what drove me to work tirelessly in network marketing—thus, the basis for this book. I'm not going to load you up with a lot of history here, but I'll note two references to the origins of "fortune" that you may not be familiar with. (For those who are, kudos for the wicked knowledge!)

In medieval and ancient philosophy, the Wheel of Fortune, or *Rota Fortunae*, is a symbol of the nature of Fate. The wheel belongs to the goddess, Fortuna, who randomly spins it, changing the positions of those on the wheel: some suffer great misfortune, others gain windfalls. The metaphor became popular in the Middle Ages as a common image in manuscripts and other media: Fortuna, often blindfolded, turns a large wheel of the sort used in watermills, to which kings and other powerful figures are attached.

In a completely different part of the world, pre-modern Japan, you have the presence of the Seven Gods of Fortune, thought to collectively possess the perfect virtues of longevity, fortune, popularity, sincerity, kindness, dignity, and magnanimity. For some, the worship of these gods is even more pronounced due to the importance of number seven in Japan.

I use these two examples of interpretations around fortune because as you read and internalize the principles of *Between Fear and Fortune*, I would like for you to define fortune on your own terms. If I put the combination of my career and the thousands of people I have worked with over the years under a microscope, I see fortune consisting of love, health, freedom, time, community, travel, service, substance, assets. I see vitality. I also see a long road of accountability. Accountability is a theme that will be reinforced throughout, with advice for building your level of accountability.

Will you worship a goddess or god of fortune, answering to their demands (okay, real or imagined!), or will you become your own fortune teller and live life on your own terms? We will search for your truth together, so be prepared for more questions. These questions are meant for you to keep your mind zinging and will be related to principles and advice I offer, not meant as arbitrary chit-chat. Anyone who has worked with me knows that everything I do is backed by a positive intention and walking the talk. Your answers will not be judged by me (I don't have that kind of telepathic power!), nor should you ridicule yourself if you know in your gut that the answer to a question doesn't reflect you doing your best. But do assess what you may need to change or improve. Without truth, you cannot reconcile…with yourself or others. Proper conditioning goes beyond the body.

Choices may have numerous ingredients to mix and stir, but in the end, they all come down to fear or fortune. My hope is that this guide both reminds you that you do have choices and steers you toward your own fortune in some small way.

PART I.

MIND MARRIES MONEY AND LIVES HAPPILY EVER AFTER

"The cave you
fear to enter
holds the
treasures you seek."

—JOSEPH CAMPBELL

CHAPTER 1

THE BUSINESS MODEL THAT CHANGED MY LIFE

I was looking for something. I was comfortable yet slightly disillusioned. I was grateful yet really ambitious. I was hard-working yet I didn't feel my rewards matched my skill set and my ability to achieve.

I'm not saying I was better than what I was. I just knew I wanted to impact more lives and earn more income.

In all my twenty-seven years, I had never heard the term, network marketing, despite this business model being around since 1963 with Mary Kay, now a $3.25 billion company. In fact, I had been enrolled as a brand partner with my company for about a month before I heard of network marketing from the late, great Jim Rohn CD on building your network marketing business. You will hear me quote Jim Rohn numerous times in this book. He started off in a network marketing company and went onto become one of the best thought leaders and philosophers of our time, mentoring people like Darron Hardy and Tony Robbins.

It's truly amazing to think someone you will never meet can have such an impact on your life. I must have listened to his CD 10,000 times, as it's timeless and still relevant today. Apart from the product I aligned myself with, the most appealing thing about this whole concept was the ability to generate income twenty-four hours a day across the globe. That was what was missing in my life. A way to build income when I was asleep. A way to grow something that will grow itself, too. A way to help and inspire people around the world—because I was fed up with linear income and owning a job simply trading time for money.

The *first element* to any successful business is the retail element and your first job, as was mine, is to retail the product and to grow a customer base. You take the product, find out what it does for you and build your story around your journey of change.

The *second element* of the business model is to convert

your happy customers into brand partners, or distributors, if we are using old-school terms. I would say eight to ten times, the best brand partners come from your customer base. Why? They have a natural love for the product and have already been recommending it and sharing their story without being signed up yet. It's just a natural transition. You take a product; you like it and you naturally tell people about it.

That said, I know many things in life is about selling or is transactional, so I'm not going to try to tell you this is not sales. However, the most successful people get really good at adding value, promoting and recommending—especially using social media. Human beings have been promoting and recommending stuff for centuries. I dare to say the first cavemen that discovered fire told the other cavemen about it before it spread by word of mouth and demonstration from tribe to tribe. It's human nature to share things that add value to our lives. We can't help ourselves from raving about products we love. (I'd like to think you're going to do the same with this book. Read it, get value from it and recommend it to someone else!)

The *third element* to our business model is networking. The clue is in the name. You have to grow a network. What makes it easier to grow a network than using the power of an online social network? I would even go as far to say this is now a "social network marketing business".

Global lockdown and quarantine events as a result of the

coronavirus have shown the power of building business using social media and online technology. This is an industry that's absolutely thriving because due to redundancies, job losses and a challenging landscape for traditional businesses.

I mean, think about this: You can choose to build a business in Singapore. Go onto social media and start to search for people, create contact with them and introduce them to your product or opportunity. This can all be done from your smart phone from your sofa in your pajamas, or at the airport while you're waiting to board a flight—even at 38,000 feet you get WiFi now, so there really isn't an excuse!

Every Monday, I go around the world using Zoom. I go to:

- Australia, 10:30 a.m.
- United Arab Emirates
- United States, by 6:00 p.m.
- Finland
- UK and Ireland, by 8:00 p.m.

What a business! And what a time to be alive to take advantage of this amazing technology.

The *fourth element* to the business is teaching. Again, the social media and technology tools we have are crucial for this. But your job is to teach your new team members how to do what you did. Get this part right and you have cracked it. Then you just have to keep repeating these key elements day in-day out, week in-week out, month after month, year after year, and for me now, decade after decade.

When you get it right, here is what it should look like:

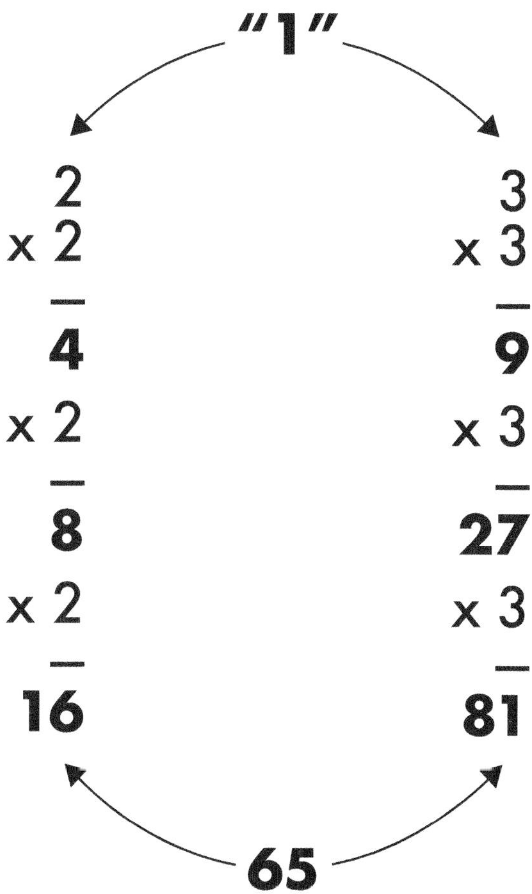

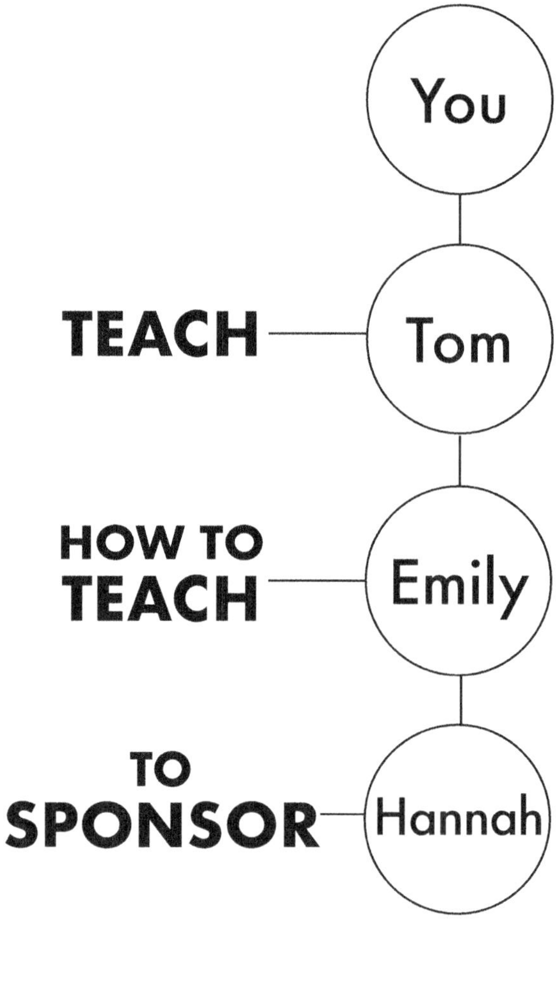
You
TEACH
Tom
HOW TO
TEACH
Emily
TO
SPONSOR
Hannah

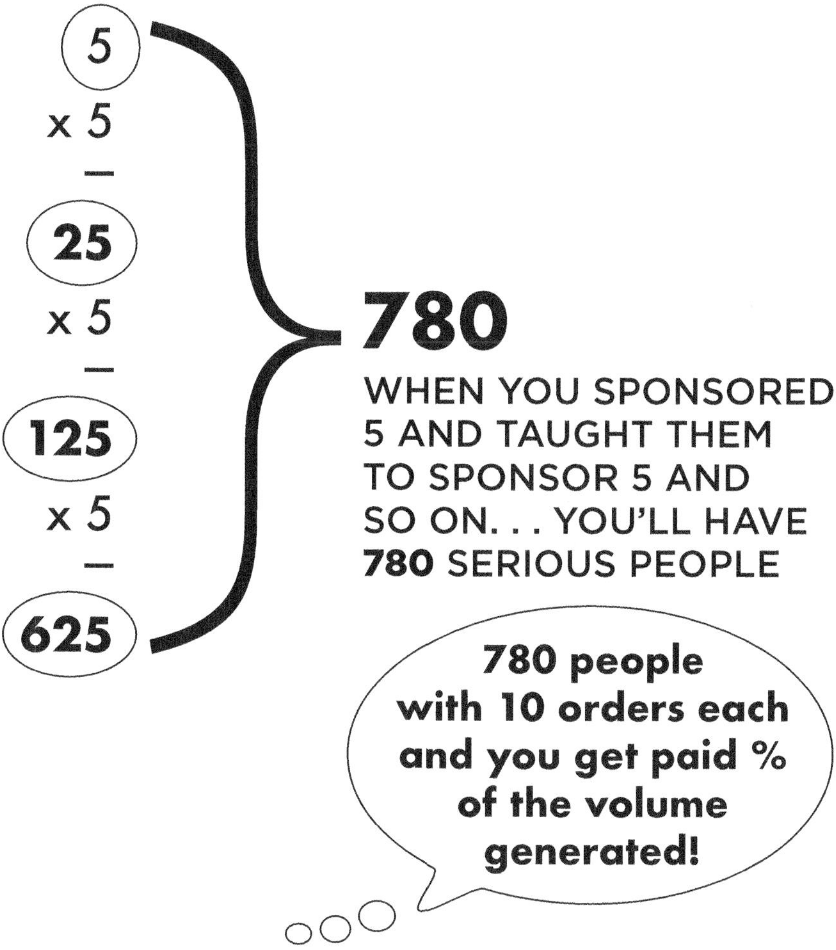

I remember seeing these diagrams unfold in front of my very eyes. I also remember teaching the system before it had started working for me. But one day, I was discussing how well the business was growing with a team member. We had just finished a training in front of a room of about 350 people.

"You kept saying this was going to happen," she said.

If you make a friend], then meet their friends. Five people join and they bring their friends, and so on and so on. It was surreal to see it play out in front of my eyes the concept excited me from day one. In fact, every time I see those numbers duplicate, I get a rush of adrenaline. Since then, I proved it works in multiple countries, too. In fact, it will work anywhere you have an amazing product and ambitious, teachable people. What I love about this is it's a lot of people doing a little bit: 780 active brand partners that enroll 10 new customers each month is 7,800 new customers in your organization of which you get paid a percentage of the volume of orders.

J. Paul Getty said, "I'd rather have 1% of the effort of 100 men than 100% of my own effort."

Now, that doesn't mean you don't give 100%. But ask yourself this question. Where is your 100% going? At the time my 100% was going into my personal training business, which was linear income. When I stopped, it stopped. As soon as I discovered the business model of network marketing, I knew it was all effort related! If I worked hard and found other ambitious people who wanted to work hard, then we would have expediential growth.

"This looks like a pyramid scheme to me," I've heard. I debated long and hard about even mentioning this because

I feel it's not really as relevant as it used to be. However, this book is to show people the truth about the industry and the business model. So, you may be a reader who's not actually involved in the business. Maybe you are new to this industry and have been posed this question by friends or parents, so I thought I would give you the answer. I also wanted to remind people that this is the best business model in the world for ordinary people to create an extraordinary life…if they want to. I think it's only right that we remind ourselves what an incredible business this is.

Pyramids schemes are illegal, but ironically, most companies and organizations around the world are structured like pyramids. Think of the military forces, the government, the supermarket, the hotel chain. Your favorite sports team. The guy at the top makes most of the money, and the CEO and the guys at the lower levels work the same hours and earn less. In your normal job, do you have someone above you to report to? Yes! Do they make more income than you? Yes. Do they have someone to report to who makes more money than them? Yes. This continues until you make it as CEO.

I remember my dad saying to me, "I know about those things—the guy at the top makes all the money. You're just making him rich!"

My reply was, "It sounds like your job."

Having started right at the bottom of the marketing plan

and working my way to the top position, I can assure you the guy at the top doesn't do nothing and make all the money. The person at the top climbed his way all the way up there investing, effort, time and energy. I can also share with you that I've made more money than the people who were above me and that I've had people in my organization also out-earn me.

For me, it really is the perfect business model. No stock, no staff, no delivery. No invoicing or money collection.

If you're looking for a get-rich scheme or way to make money by doing nothing, you might as well stop reading now because you're in the wrong place with the wrong mindset. But if you have ambition, an incredible work ethic and a burning desire to achieve more and become more, you are totally in the right place.

True champions

aren't always the ones

that win, but those with

the most guts.

—MIA HAMM

CHAPTER 2

DESIRE IS NOT DESTINY

Searching for Your Truth

How did you sleep last night?

What was the first thing you did this morning?

What did you eat for breakfast?

Did you set goals for the day or week?

My parents were always working. My mum worked in telecommunications and worked nights. I remember being a kid and my mum always working yet somehow around to take care of me, too. My dad was successful working fulltime in a company and worked from home most of my younger adult life, which was great in many ways, but not when it came to be bunking off school. Both of my grandparents worked. Needless to say, you won't find any slackers on my family tree. I can really now see where my insane work ethic comes from even though if you spoke to my parents when I was a teen, they would have said I was lazy. Knowing what I know now, I was defiantly lost in the mix of trying to find something I really wanted to do.

I think sometimes we get stuck in between this mindset of, "well, this is my dream and I really want to persue it and I'm willing to do whatever it takes" and "this will do, it's not my dream but it pays the bills and it's not too difficult". How many people do you know that really love what they do and wake up with a passion for life and their job every single day? It's a small percentage. That's why there is such a live-for-the-weekend mentality and a fixation on one big vacation a year.

Author Robert Kiyosaki talks about the 40/40/40 law in his book, *Rich Dad Poor Dad*. Work 40 hours a week, for 40 years of your life and retire on 40% of your income. Forty years of your life doing a job you're not really loving is not really a life. In this current climate, are jobs that secure? Is a retirement plan secure?

I remember being standing behind an elderly gentleman in a store. I would guess his age to be about 70 years old. He was saying to the shop attendant he had just finished an eight-hour shift at a factory. On the one hand, I thought, *wow, that's incredible and I tip my hat to him.* Then I felt so sorry for him and thought, *this guy should be sitting on the dock of the bay, with a nice glass of red and the sun on his back.* Not braving the freezing cold Manchester weather as he walked back to his car after working the day shift on a Sunday.

You can learn a lot from other people's lives, decisions and choices. I would have loved to ask that guy some questions to find out what led him to that situation. But I guess you can fill in the blanks. Money mismanagement, no mentor or blueprint to follow, not having the courage to persue his dream.

Network marketers in their seventies are the total opposite. I went to a leadership convention in Long Beach, California back in 2013 and I had never been so inspired in my life. It was like a scene from the classic movie, "Cocoon" (where an alien spacecraft lands in a retirement village and delivers the fountain of youth). Here, seventy-year-olds, with beaming smiles, glowing skin and a spring in their step had more energy than most people in their twenties. Talk about a lust for life! They were fit, ambitious and still working on their passion and purpose.

You can fill in the blanks here, too. They had the courage to follow an opportunity, they found a blueprint and mentor. They, just like the factory worker, had an incredible work ethic. But they had a better vehicle to take their work ethic into a growing and abundant lifestyle business.

Maybe the old guy I encountered at the shop never heard about network marketing, but you won't have that excuse. You've found the treasure map. You just have to follow it and your fortune awaits.

I have played both sides of this coin and have done a wide range of jobs. From working as a bartender in the local town hall, to working as a mailman delivering letters. I worked as a special needs assistant at a school for about three years, which was actually one of the most rewarding jobs I've ever done. I also helped out in the afterschool club with the sole mission of getting the kids away from the computer screen and outside into the fresh air to play sports. There were some great lessons in there for me, too. Ultimately, I was successful in making the computers redundant, as most of the kids fell in love with outdoor games and sports. Thereafter, I stumbled into the fitness industry.

Have I always had that entrepreneurial spirit? I guess so, as

I was always involved in selling things at school —including gardening services during the summer holidays and designer clothes in class as a kid. I've got some hilarious stories around that, but maybe that can wait for another book.

I always wanted to earn my own money. I operated the toughest paper route in the neighborhood, with loads of hills, because it was the one nobody wanted to do, and it paid the most. I guess this was an early sign that I was prepared to do what other people weren't so I could have and do what other people couldn't. I had a business-moneymaking mindset and never ran out of ideas. It wasn't just about money though; it was more about creativity and growth. Two things I love. I didn't have any formal influences back then. I just did it because it was fun.

When I first met my mentor, Alex Hamer-Webb, at an event, I had just earned around $28 dollars from my first network marketing pay cheque. Having heard his speech, I approached him at the end of the meeting. He stood in a cream-colored suit and had a look and voice like Morgan Freeman but a Manchester version. He looked the part and talked with such conviction about residual income, building a global business and living in the sunshine whenever he wanted to. I asked, "Can you really make money in this thing?" I was the total opposite of looking the part and I had driven forty-five minutes to this meeting from my gym after training clients from 8:00 a.m. on a Saturday morning. My hair was all over the place and I was in my gym gear.

Alex always talked about finding rough diamonds and polishing them up. That's certainly what he must have seen in me because I wasn't shining that morning. He gave me his phone number and said to call him on Monday for the opportunity to work together for ninety days.

I understood that chance was possible for me because he had been doing it for twenty years. He believed in me. He believed in my future. He wanted to help me increase my belief. He also knew to make it fun along the way. My trajectory wouldn't be easy, but nothing ever worth it is, contrary to what a lot of people think…or report. I love the Big Sean line, "It took me ten years to become an overnight success."

LOOKING PAST DARK HEADLINES

When you are building a business, initially you may toe the line between madness and clarity. By madness, I mean the chaos that sometimes comes with learning new things, executing new tasks, pushing yourself beyond limits, the pressure you put on yourself to succeed and getting past the noise.

The great thing about our industry is that anyone can join. Your past, race or religion do not matter. If you want to join and change your life, you can. The risk that comes with this level of openness is that anyone can join. In any industry there are people who stick to the protocol and the rules and regulations set by the governing body. However, there are bad doctors, bad mechanics, people willing to break and bend the rules. Our industry is even more vulnerable to a mix of bad players. It's heavy on social media and it's very people-centric in the chain. There can be false income claims, false product claims, people that take credit card details, people who make a splash and a lot of money and then they don't look after clients or people they brought in.

There is a hell of a lot of passion and enthusiasm in our industry and it's built on excitement, especially at the start. I remember seeing this for the first time and I had hope. I saw a future for myself. I was so excited and wanted to tell everyone I found the winning lottery ticket. So, when there is excitement, people can and do exaggerate. People can easily fall into the trap of hyping up a lot of things, making irresponsible claims or social media posts and giving a great industry a bad name.

I've never been a big believer of "fake it until you make it". Don't get me wrong. I love and use visualization, and vision boards are a big part of my training. But telling people you're doing better than you are and false income stories I just can't accept. I honestly think people feel this business and people can feel if you're telling the truth or not.

I would much rather say, "I've just joined. I'm super excited. I've seen the marketing plan and it's really impressive. I've also seen the people who have worked their way to the top and I know I can do it, too. I'm not there yet, but I'm going to be. I would love you to take a look because it would be so cool to work with you on this," versus, "I only joined up last Tuesday and now, I'm a seven-figure earner."

You can still be excited about it and paint a picture of what your life will be like without having to tell tales and make false claims. Lets face it we will never keep all the bad players out, but which industry does? For example, there can be high poaching element. New companies launch and target other network marketers and try to disrupt or take leaders. We know this is the same in a lot of industries, but it's even more disruptive in network marketing. It reminds me of the scene in "A Bug's Life" where the ants work all year to build up stocks of food and just before the harvest, the grasshoppers invade and steal or poach all their stuff.

The first time it happened to me and my business, it was tough. My advice on determining the integrity of the group or team you want to join is, do your research, really look into the situation and question people's intentions and promises. Focus on what you love about your business other than money. In my opinion, sticking around the people you built with from the start is so powerful, credible and authentic.

Those friendships and relationships can last forever and will outlast any short and fast hit of income. I'm not saying you shouldn't change companies if you have to or if things aren't a good fit for you anymore. Of course, you have to do what you feel is right for you and your family. But really think about your values and your reputation.

"John," you say, "this can happen in every profession." Bad blood, bad medicine. Sure, but what about when media giants like BBC disperse bad press you either have to decipher or ignore—particularly in your "infant" stage?

I read the negative articles about my business and about the model and industry before I got into the industry. It did bother me, of course; however, opinions are like belly buttons—everyone has one but they're not that useful! I thought, *if Coke is still around and McDonald's is thriving with negative press, my business can do it too.* Especially when you look at the positive stories surrounded by many products in our industry. I have thousands of examples of how products have changed lives. Real stories of people who have changed their lives within the business. Since 2013, in Europe alone, approximately 400,000 have joined the business, so take that, BBC!

Some have left the industry but changed their mindset amidst the process. We often say this is a personal development course disguised as a business. As you grow, your business grows. You will always get negativity coming from one corner. Unfortunately, it sells and spreads sometimes. People have their own agenda, whether it's another company competing or an individual who has been burned in the past.

When people don't succeed in a goal they set, they find it hard to take responsibility. It's so easy to say "it didn't work for me" when the truth is you didn't do the work. You can't blame the dumbbells or the treadmill for not being in shape. The weights will always be there, but nobody will lift them for you. It's the same with business and especially network marketing. People can join, but their expectations don't match their work ethic and consistency. So, they join and do a little, and doing a little doesn't really yield much results. Because there is little result, they do less again. Less again leads to less results and they've joined and given up within a four-week window.

The ones who give up and quit then write their blame list but fail to include themselves on it!

Negativity can also leak into the industry. One guy posted so much negativity around the industry, but we discovered he had never actually been a part of it. Someone confronted him about it, and he said bottom line, that he hated his ex-wife, who was a part of the industry, and he didn't want her to succeed. He wanted to "destroy" her. That's a pretty ugly situation. It happens, unfortunately.

My belief from over the past decade is too strong to let negativity overturn it. Everything is balanced. Manchester United is the most popular football club in the UK, but it's also the most hated. When you rise to the top, someone will inevitably try to shoot you down. The best players always get booed by the opposing fans. There is jealousy, especially on social media. People can share opinions without having any awareness or real knowledge. Those opinions in the same space as someone who just may be knowledgeable, and fair carry the same weight to a viewer.

I'll give you an example from the beauty world. The cosmetics industry, which is dominated by the United States, bringing in revenue of about $70 billion, does an exorbitant amount of business through individual reps and social media. Well, one company has eight different presenter statuses in a commissions-based model. Presenters buy and sell through social media and usually Facebook. Its reputation is a mixed bag, but numerous people, including stay-at-home moms have made a living and obtained freedom from working this commission-based model and some have just become happy customers of the product. It's not for everyone. Is anything?

Now, if you're discouraged from pursuing your dreams when you hear negative comments or skim bad press, I really want you to think about what you're made of. Fear or fortune? You steer your future and live in your own skin. Only you can know what is "right" for you.

Follow soccer? It's okay if you don't, but it's still worth sharing something about Mia Hamm, who is considered to be soccer's leading international scorer, male or female, with 158 goals. The world's largest sporting event for women, the 1999 World Cup, was built on her reputation, as was the Women's United Soccer Association, a professional league that followed. It's important to know one thing about her back story: She didn't wake up with a soccer jersey on, wealth, and accolades one day! In the early days of the women's national team, Hamm and her teammates played in obscurity, living on candy bars in China and lacking running water and electricity in Haiti. During that time, it's widely reported that she also received negative messages about performance as a girl and that the World Cup was only a dream.

I imagine what sacrifices Hamm made to become such an outstanding athlete and the world's top scorer.

SIGNATURE SACRIFICES

You're either making decisions and investing time and energy into things that are taking you towards your goal or further away from your goal. We only have twenty-four hours per day and a certain amount of energy units per day. Where you invest them is crucial.

Think about your signature sacrifices—not just any and every sacrifice you need to make to succeed, but the hardest ones to make. Those that have been irking you for some time or keep popping up in your life. Write them down somewhere you will see frequently. It's okay if you don't make the sacrifice straight away, but awareness is quite empowering. It's like a lightbulb in your mind to activate an action step towards the right choice! The beauty is that every step counts.

In my early days, I needed to see from a mindset point of view that if I continued to do what I was doing, I was always going to get the same outcome. I didn't want to be an "old personal trainer," doing the same thing for years and years. I wanted more! I wanted to get long-term benefits of creating this sort of business. Rather than watching soccer (sorry, Mia!) or going out with friends on weekends, I would go to professional development conferences and work on my network marketing business. I would sacrifice short-term income from clients. I had the option to earn 200 pounds for a day's personal training or head down to Mastermind Weekends for my business. I grew that long-term vision.

I remember one day, getting invited to attend a workshop with a seven-figure income earner who had flown in from LA. It meant canceling a full day in the gym. Spending money on filling the tank and potentially getting home late that night after outrageously bad traffic. I arrived to pick up my team member at 7:00 a.m. from his house. He didn't answer his phone. Eventually, I got through.

"Where are you?" I asked.

"I'm in bed hungover. I only got in at 5:00 a.m. I will come to the next one."

There won't be a next one, I thought. I knew this was a sliding doors moment for him. He rolled over and went to sleep on his dreams. I put on "The Black Album" by Jay-Z, turned up the volume and drove closer to realizing my dream.

Four years later, while in Manchester on a shopping spree for a convention I was attending in Long Beach, I bumped into the same guy. I was right—there had not been a "next one "for him. He gave up soon after missing that event. "Wow, John, I just gotta say congratulations, you've done amazing. It's great to see all the success you're having on social media." I felt like saying "it could have been you too," but I just didn't have the heart to say I told you so. People let little things cheat them out of big opportunities and there is nothing we can do to stop it.

In my opinion, or certainly in my career, there has been no bigger thief of time than alcohol. I've seen it in myself over the years and also in others. I frequently gave up alcohol for sustained periods just so I would be totally present in my business. The reason I mention alcohol a few times is straightforward: Not only is alcohol extremely accessible; drinking it is just as socially acceptable as drinking tea or water! Champagne signifies celebration. Wine signifies a dinner party or wind-down at the end of the day, and beer signifies a sporting event with the fellas. But we all know that consuming it can have negative consequences. As I said, the biggest thief of time I've ever seen is alcohol. How many days have you lost over the years through drinking, being hungover or just operating at 45% of your capacity?

There is a great freedom and clarity in sustained periods of sobriety. I'm six months sober at the writing of this book, which has allowed me to get into the shape of my life, the productivity of my life and I've been able to double my business.

We all have the power to choose creativity over alcohol. We all have a kryptonite or nemesis. Maybe it's scrolling and rolling on social media. Maybe it's drugs. Maybe its binging on sport or box sets. Or overthinking. But your units of time and energy are going somewhere, and the impact will show up in the positive or negative.

Even though your brain is not a muscle, chemically you can tire it out by thinking too much. "We are not wired to use the 'higher order executive function' all the time," says Melanie Greenberg, Ph.D., author of *The Stress-Proof*

Brain. While "higher order executive function" can include obvious tasks like taking a test, it can also comprise a combination of smaller challenges, like processing a lot of new information coming at you at once.

When your brain is dealing with an ongoing supply of new information, it must put energy into every decision, which overuses that executive function and can cause mental fatigue. And if we're looking to be top players, we always have to weigh taking chances that may set us back in our attention span, hours we keep, and goals we achieve.

Having a work ethic, getting up one or two hours earlier to get things done, also became a mirror for me. Fighting fatigue, I would stay up to complete tasks. I remember my mum urging me to go to bed. "You look exhausted!" she would say. Everything I did in those early days was hardcore effort, which came first. It was always about driving my business momentum.

It's vital that you speak to potential clients and team members when you're in a peak state. Also be aware of how much personal development you do and at what times. Don't fall into the trap of thinking personal development is building your business. You need to stay focused on those income-producing activities. There is a sweet spot for everything, so choose your time wisely and structure your day accordingly. Set yourself up for success. If you know

Monday is the best day to do calls, then nothing should get in the way of that. If you know Sunday is the best day to put time into your family, then commit to that time. As Jim Rohn would say, "Don't take your briefcase to the beach and don't fool around on serious business-building days." Get the work done and live in the present.

My business is really special in that I diversified and included network marketing into my own personal business model, then skyrocketed with that. It's important to know that I'm not just about the glamor. I work the business every day. It's about purposeful action every single day. Sometimes, that is not the story that gets associated with network marketing.

I have a saying: "Never have a zero." Some days will be 10/10 days! Everything runs right when you're super productive and you kick ass! Some days you might get a solid 8; some days are 5 or a 6! Some might be a day of mishaps, distractions and demotivation, but you have to ensure to never have a zero day where you go to bed having done nothing to water and nurture your future.

Since I started out as an entrepreneur, I've done something every single day to grow my business and my brand. I've never had a zero. I want my story to be a hero's journey, and I want you to own yours as one, too.

Wheel of Accountability

AVOID TEMPTATION!
Empathize with your future self.
Make manageable goals.

"If you want to be happy, set a goal that commands your thoughts, liberates your energy and inspires your hopes."

—ANDREW CARNEGIE

CHAPTER 3

MISSION ON THE MOUNTAINTOP

Searching for Your Truth

When was the last time you thought about your purpose?

Do you serve others often?

Do you loathe or love looking in the mirror?

Do you tend to conform to patterns or are you open?

It may not be exciting to give up alcohol for ninety days or chocolate for a few weeks. In fact, it may seem damned painful to even think about it but consider that personal development goes hand in hand with fitness, productivity and business.

In my Dream Chasers mastermind group, we focus on what I believe are the three key pillars to success: Business, Body and Brain. These three pillars or concepts feed each other. When one or two are neglected, then it can have a direct correlation on all three. I know this from personal experience and from working with team members.

Why is it that when you do less, you feel more tired and less productive? Yet you get a solid workout in or go for a brisk walk and you raise your heart rate, your hormones kick in and you start to feel good and more creative. This has a positive effect on your business.

Feed your body great foods with live enzymes and drinks that hydrate and nourish your body and you will feel alive. Feed it dead food and toxins, and you will be intoxicated and sluggish. Feed your brain positive stories, uplifting messages, and surround yourself with blue-sky thinkers and you will think happier thoughts, see more possibilities and grow into a great leader who overcomes challenges and creates many success stories. Buy into negative headlines, stay around the doom and gloom merchants and waste time and energy being unproductive, and you will see that show up in your body, your mindset and your business.

Growing your bicep or booty in the gym is the same as growth in your mindset. Do the work and you build the muscle! The hard-knocks truth is that if you eat certain foods and make daily bad choices, you might have a heart attack, you might get cancer. Most illness and disease are linked to lifestyle choices. And it's increasing in this world of fast-food and instant gratification. That's not the line of thinking that I want to explore or take you down with. I'm an optimist and prefer to show you a better way than show you that you're stuck in a mess. I don't prefer harsh language or medical instructions that sound preachy. I prefer to see everything as personal development and choices. You have choices to see your food and drink environment as irreplaceable desires or tools for the way you live.

If you put diesel in a jet fuel engine, you're not going to perform well. My philosophy is around business, body and brain. To have a successful business, you need to look after your body and your brain. What you put into your body will dictate how you feel. If you put alcohol into your body, you get a comedown the next day. It slows you down. You get negative thoughts. You get the beer fear. For me, giving up alcohol was a direct show of discipline because I just couldn't afford one day of lounging on the couch and watching garbage on the television.

If you're not batting 100 percent, how do you expect your team to? Creativity flows from this *one simple change* of more green vegetables on that plate. Food is your mood, and motion creates emotion.

If you want to kill motivation, eat and drink the wrong things. Have you stopped to think that what we eat can dictate what is going on in our brain? Really study that. I confess, I love Golden Grahams, but the way you start your day determines the rest of your day and week, so I always start my day with healthy choices of amazing plant-based protein, low GI carbohydrates, the essence of nutrients going through my bloodstream every day.

People see a spring in your step. They want that! Make it sexy: Put the colors in, such as blueberries and raspberries. Blend it up and showcase it on social media. Others want that! Use your diet to serve your brain.

If you want to perform, you need to put good stuff in your body. We're designed to move as human beings so having that hour of power in the gym or taking a forty-minute walk can fulfill that focus and releasing those happy hormones. In fact, I would get my best ideas in the sauna and have to get out and write things down!

If you're listening to the news all the time, you're not in control of what is put in your brain. If you're around negative people, you won't be inspired to keep going so you need to be around good people. You need to read the right books. Fitness feeds into mindset. Mindset feeds into fitness.

I was listening to an audio book once late at night and my dad came into my bedroom and told me to "turn that rubbish down—you're brainwashed!" I was listening to Jim Rohn to close up my day working on my subconscious level of thinking while it played when I was sleeping. I needed to be positive in the here and now, so I even took out all my favorite music from the car and only listened to high-energy, motivational content that would get me into a peak state. This is especially important when living with family members who don't get it or see what you see.

Aspire to be the product of the product or service you are selling—the best version of yourself and in love with that product or service.

Sacrifices and effort require time and energy into the right things. As of this writing, I attended a leaders' retreat in Portugal. Do you know how many times I heard the message to work consistently, day after day? Every single person who pronounced this looked the part of effort, with professional presence and energy. There simply are no substitutes or short cuts.

Let's get away from this bullshit of network marketing: "Sign up, do nothing and then earn loads of money!" The reason it gets a bad reputation is that people are sold the dream without work ethic. My business is all effort-related. In fact, I'm working harder on myself and my business than ever before. The other side of it is you need a bit of blind faith. You need to keep going, keep faith and maintain your work ethic. Keep planting the seeds and watering them daily, even when nothing seems to be growing. Remember, lush trees grow underground first. You don't see the roots develop or taking shape, but they are. Others may go down that rabbit hole of negativity if they get a "no." People need to hold themselves accountable. It's about effort, energy and making the right choices.

For all you extraverts out there, I love you, but passion is empty without action! Instead of continually telling your social media how this is your time—"watch me now, just you wait and see"—why not keep quiet and do the work? Tell me what you've done, not what you're continually going to do. This whole strategy of post on social media, do a little work for a day or two, then start again, doesn't serve you.

I have sacked clients after seeing their food diaries. They would bring me a list of what they've eaten that week with a laugh. Their goal was more important to me than it was to them. Is it really funny to give up? To be that constant quitter?

When I became a personal trainer and earned my qualifications, it was a risk. I had to pay rent at the gym. My first month, I had to earn $800 just to give to the gym. There was a recession and everyone who wasn't an entrepreneur told me not to do it. But everything is about systems; just learn them and implement them. The company I signed up with gave us a manual to work through and learn. I had never done sales before.

My mum said, "All you can do is follow the system they've given you to the best of your ability. If it doesn't work, then at least you can say you did everything they told you to do."

It's a numbers game now, and it was back then, opening up conversations, giving free education, taster sessions. I was in the gym from 6:00 in the morning to 10:00 at night. I literally said "hello" to every single person in that gym. You have to SHOW UP, not just appear in the doorway. It's exactly the same in your network marketing business and showing up on your social media platforms. You have to be the go-to person and be the first in someone's thoughts when they think about your product benefits or your business.

If you're moaning and you're a negative Nelly, people don't want to be near you. Authenticity is huge in network marketing. People think they have to promote perfect lives in social media. If your baby is waking you up every thirty minutes and you've hardly slept but still managed to make it to the gym, share that. Your long-term future depends on this type of effort, and it's not easy. There are challenges. Share that. Sharing not only positions you for additional connections in your network; it builds your brand and shows that you are vulnerable and human like the rest of us.

People are inspired by human stories!

Polish discus thrower Piotr Malachowski won a silver medal in Rio. Almost immediately, however, he put that medal up for auction to help fund a cancer treatment for a three-year-old boy. According to ESPN's Darren Rovell, Malachowski's goal was to raise enough money to ensure Olek Szymanski "could get surgery for his retinoblastoma in New York to try to save the child's eyesight."

Rovell reported that Polish foundation Siepomaga had raised about a third of the $126,000 needed for the surgery, and Malachowski hoped to raise the rest with the action. Shortly after the auction began, Malachowski announced on Facebook, per Rovell, that a wealthy Polish couple had committed to covering the remaining amount required.

Wheel of Accountability

YOUR THOUGHTS CREATE REALITY.
Better thoughts help you design a better reality.

"Between stimulus and response, there is a space. In that space is our **power to choose our response.** In our response lies **our growth** and **our freedom.**"

—VICKTOR EMIL FRANKL

CHAPTER 4

FREE AND STABLE?

Searching for Your Truth

How do you define freedom?

How do you define stability?

Do you have regular routines that you follow religiously?

If you could describe your future with one or two words, what would it or they be?

People get disconnected. They lose structure. You're joining your plan B business to acquire freedom. I was excited to travel the world, get on planes, stay in hotels. I just want to say there is a flashing light, so have some awareness.

All distractions are equal. I can remember team members getting married and they lost focus in their business. Moving to a new house and lost focus in their business. Getting divorced and losing focus in their business. Having a baby and losing focus in their business. I also know people who have had those distractions go on and they have grown through some really tough times. One of our team members used the pain of losing her mum as her fuel to grow to a pinnacle leadership position. Others have used break-ups to grow and pregnancy to fuel their performance.

Just like other people before me and alongside me, I let success become a distraction, especially traveling. What happened with me is that I was drinking all the time and ordering room service at 3:00 in the morning. My peak would hit at 8:00 p.m. and I would be on fire. I couldn't come down from speaking at events and then going to nightclubs where I would be out until the early hours. Then I would sleep in and go to the next town to do another event. I would be exhausted, and I'd tell myself that I needed to have a good time because people had come for this and expected it. I would convince myself that if we didn't go out and have a great team night out, then people would eventually slow down and lose interest.

I remember flying back to Manchester from an event in Switzerland. We also watched the England soccer team from the corporate box. The good times flowed. It was an incredible experience yet the next day, I had a speaking event in Manchester and then Liverpool the following day. Instead of getting an early night and putting some good stuff into my body, I showed up to the event in a low energy-exhausted state. And I felt like I was letting people down. They were expecting a show. A business pitch of motivation and inspiration. The only way I could get back to that peak state was having a few beers before the event. We partied hard after and repeated the same formula. But it was unsustainable and emitted the wrong kind of energy.

Like everything in life and especially in this business the stories we tell ourselves have a dramatic impact on many areas. I vowed to be totally honest when writing this book so that's why I share this stuff. I do this in the hope it may save you from making similar mistakes. The truth was and is, your team growth is not defined by a night out. If anything has proved that, it's pandemic-driven lockdown and quarantine. We've had no physical face-to-face events in 2020 yet business is stratospheric.

Why did I choose to go down this path? What you think you want is not always what you need. It was a far cry from my old life as a personal trainer and bootcamp owner where I would start my first camps at 6:30 in the morning and then end at 8:30 p.m., working Monday to Sunday and being totally rigid in my structure. Never missing a session. Even the thought of letting people down now or having them standing waiting outside my gym in the rain gives me anxiety and created an already pressure-laden business. So, I guess I was in search for freedom with no responsibility.

This false freedom was a totally different life. It didn't serve me. It took me a while to realize what I really *needed.* I had conflicting thoughts and concepts of freedom and stability and I would urge you to examine yours before making any big decisions.

When some people have more time, unfortunately, they become lazier and get distracted. Busy people get stuff done. When athletes retire, they lose structure and gain pounds! Some people are not meant to be entrepreneurs and don't have the foundation it takes to literally build their own business. They are building on quicksand. Having come through this part of my journey with many lessons, I know have a new concept of freedom.

PURPOSEFUL FREEDOM

I first heard of a similar concept around 2012 when I heard someone talk about their perfect day. They had built a business that allowed them to live their perfect day. Yet their business activity was part of their perfect day. I remember asking myself what my perfect day would look like. What country would I be in? What would be my morning routine? Where would I put my energy? Who would I be with? What would my afternoon look like?

I then started to visualize what my perfect day would look like. I could see the movie play out in my mind. Having a nice coffee in the morning on the balcony looking out over the ocean view. Getting a morning workout in. Doing some work on content creation or a power hour on my business. Breaking my fast with a superfood green smoothie and an omelet. Maybe taking a stroll in the sunshine. Then coming back to do a bit more work on my business in the afternoon. Getting that second coffee in while I read a chapter of a book. Then getting ready for my evening calls when I share the product and the opportunity. Wrapping up the call to enjoy the sunset with a chamomile tea or a non-alcoholic beer on a school night. That was my dream back then and that was just one version of my perfect day. Obviously, you can add things in (BBQs, surfing, playing tennis, afternoon at the beach club listening to some funky house, enjoying a nice meal with your partner down by the fishing village… you get the idea).

My perfect day always had a few key elements: personal growth, exercise, sunshine, views and nice scenery and being with people I love and care about. And of course, building my business. I love building my business and I need to do something on it daily. It fulfills me and gives me purpose. I'm a better person when I get my business stuff done, my exercise and some form of personal development. It's there again, the Dream Chasers' philosophy of business, body and brain.

My old life as a personal trainer had certain elements, but there were some frustrations. I felt like my business growth was always stifled as I didn't have an unlimited growth business model. I had a ceiling. Only so many hours in the day and only so much space in my studio. I also had irregular income and many nights where I would wake up in cold sweats worried about money and never being able to provide for or live the life I wanted. There was almost zero sunshine. The UK weather is unpredictable. You can't plan anything because it may be sunny for a few days and then come the weekend, it will pour down. For the times we would get a nice day, I was stuck in the gym for hours on end. Then the weekend family BBQ would get cancelled because a wild, wet and windy weather front from the Atlantic would charge in.

But I used this motivation to create that lifestyle. Now I get to live that perfect day every day.

I don't care what anyone says. When you get up, open your curtains and see blue skies and sunshine, you instantly feel alive and energized. There is scientific evidence that proves this case, too. Now, we don't have the power to change the weather, but we do have the power to change where we live—especially with the network marketing business model! You will hear some stories other than mine of people who have been able to do just this.

Now, don't fall into this myth of "beach money". Beach money means living by the beach and working your business from there. Not sitting on the beach and doing nothing and making money. That's where the unfulfillment, boredom and decline creep in. Living a life of purposeful freedom is where it's at. I've done the whole party-everyday lifestyle and doing the bare minimum in terms of exercise and business. You feel so much better when you earn it, when you build it and when you stay focused on the process of growth.

The truth is we never switch off and we don't want to. We don't need to either. If you structure your perfect day, you create a life you don't need a vacation from.

In December, in our industry, some people drop down a gear and take time off. The numbers are always rubbish. But if you were a florist or owned a café, would you put the "vacation" sign on the door automatically? You always need to be ON. Doing nothing shows up later. The consistency of staying focused is key. In December, if you're being trained physically, you have to work harder. You have to fight temptation.

Freedom is not having more space to make bad choices. Everyone has a weak spot, whether it's procrastination or movie binging. We need to put a personal development slant on this. What things are you putting into your brain? Where are you putting your time and energy? Who are you hanging with? And what are they doing to you? Two favorite sayings: "You won't become a black belt hanging around with white belts." "If you want to fly with eagles, you can't run with the turkeys."

Though I emphasize using social media for the benefits of business development, connection and community, there is also a time when it does not serve you. When you are working out your struggle like the elimination of booze or sugar, or procrastination, until you have figured out the solution, work it out privately and personally. Any trip-up can only exacerbate your frustration. It can be detrimental and dangerous if you use your social media platform for accountability and recovery. Be honest with yourself. Find an accountability group outside of your work frame to step this up. I worked a lot on this behind the scenes and never posted or shared the fact I was working with coaches and delving into books and information to restructure my day, my week and my life.

When it comes to freedom and increasingly ramping up to freedom and stability, if you're not happy where you are, you need to *do* things to get you where you want to be rather than talk about it and think about it. More truth here: We all know deep down what is holding us back, whether we want to keep staring at it or not. People know when they've been inconsistent, cancelled events, missed calls and didn't show up.

You know when you've eaten yourself silly instead of working out—though you already set your goal to lose weight. Or drank so much that you miss the event or meeting. I know people who haven't gone to a business event because they were "having a bloated day" or won't share their story on a Zoom call because they haven't done their hair or makeup. I've also known people so hungover they almost didn't get their recognition on stage. I've been there myself, so there is no judgment. These are just lessons and getting to the crux of the issue helps you avoid the same pitfalls in the future—or as I'm trying to do here, help you avoid them in the first place.

Whatever the endeavor, remember why you joined in the first place. The reason I stayed in networking marketing after two years of not earning much money was challenge, growth, and friendships. I believed in the products and the business model. All the stuff I was rubbish at, the company did. The community helped me dream bigger and showed me and many others that there was room for everyone at the top and all you had to do was follow the path. I always knew there was something more for me than being a PE teacher or a personal trainer. I just had to keep working towards it.

I designed the life I wanted in my mind's eye, I put it on my vision board and thought about it every day. I went to work on myself and on the business and I turned my dream life into a reality. Now I urge you to dream up your perfect day and create it.

Need an extreme example of dreaming big?

In 2001, former Formula One driver Alex Zanardi was involved in an auto racing accident that resulted in the amputation of both his legs. Now, the Italian is a four-time Paralympic champion hand cyclist. Zanardi secured his third Paralympic gold (he won two in London in 2012) by winning the H5 time trial in Rio the day before the 15th anniversary of his crash. He was also part of the H2-H5 mixed team relay gold.

Zanardi had already fulfilled a dream. He didn't even allow such a life-altering event to stop him from dreaming again.

Wheel of Accountability

STABILITY TRUMPS UNNECESSARY DRAMA AND STRESS.

Practice deep breathing. It takes conscious effort to claim stability.

"If my future were determined just by my performance on a standardized test, I wouldn't be here.

I guarantee you that."

—MICHELLE OBAMA

CHAPTER 5

ATTACK IT AND TRACK IT!

Searching for Your Truth

Do you have laugher in your life every day?

How many colors were on your last dinner (or *supper*, depending on where you are in the world) plate?

Do you share what you are proud of with others?

Do friends think of you as being optimistic?

Raise your hand if you hated math beyond the basics, chemistry, or science that involved measuring. I feel you! Capturing data or being an information junkie isn't fun for some people. On the other hand, some people love data, numbers and the finer detail. If you're like me, you shy away from this type of stuff, but I can assure you, getting a few basics things right could make all the difference.

We have a saying in our business: It's a "*go about your business* type of business". What that means is that you build the business in and around the spare time in your day. A conversation here. A few posts there. A bit of follow-up while you're cooking the kids dinner. This is a great platform and starting point to build from, and it's the way I built my business for years. In the nooks and crannies of the day. This style of building will never leave you, by the way. You will always be switched on and you need to be; in fact, you can't help not being.

What I realized was once I took the time to actually map out my schedule and create a timetable, I would rarely stray from that structure. It became embedded into my sub-conscious. Almost like your school timetable. I would never forget a bootcamp or miss a training session and my diary came everywhere with me. Like with any good platform, you then have something to look at and build into. Where are my quiet times? When can I fit in my morning workout?

What night is best for team calls? What time do I block out a few hours to follow up?

One thing I learned early on though is that tracking is not hard if you are consistent and disciplined, with routines. For example, facing the worst scrambled eggs in my life, three times a week for three years, I fulfilled my morning networking events. I showed up to meet other business owners and exchange referrals at 6:30 a.m. Tracking was automatic since I didn't ever miss the chance of meeting someone who could potentially be a diamond in my business. Were these times sometimes awkward and clumsy? Did I arrive with the worst bedhead you've ever seen? For sure. I would hear that alarm go off and think, *what the hell am doing this for.* I would put my foot out of the bed and feel the freezing cold air. It was pitch black and usually raining outside. Most days, I had to force myself to go, but usually, it was worth it. To be fair, I'll remember those eggs doing backstroke in oil and those sausages being cooked under lights forever! Not to mention the worst coffee you've ever had.

And? These feelings or blatant resistance cannot stop you from attacking your goals.

But showing up is more than half the battle. The situation you're worried about is never as bad as you think. Yeah, it was cold, it was raining, it wasn't always value for money in terms of the referrals you would get. But if you don't go, you will never know. It always comes down to the choice of two pains: the pain of doing the work or the pain of never hitting your goals.

At the time of writing this book, a team member who I met indirectly through a networking event has just hit the pinnacle position on our leadership ladder. I went to the event one Friday morning. I honestly dragged myself there, but I met a lady named Bev, who said, "I've got the perfect person for your business." She's into my health and fitness and she's an ex-pharmaceutical research rep. That Sunday, Bev brought Sue to an event we were doing. Sue was great and joined up. Sue then introduced me to a fitness instructor named Julia, and both Sue and Julia amassed enormous business and still work closely with me to this day. Julia just hit one of our top positions.

As Steve Jobs said, "You can only line the dots up looking backwards." I'm not saying you have to go to networking breakfasts to build a business. What I am saying is that I was willing to do whatever it took in the time I had. Adopt that attitude and you will make it to the top.

In 2015, at the Birmingham NLC Convention, I remember walking out to the track, "I'm Different", opening up my speech with the words, "It pays to be different. People will tell you it's not the right thing to do; wanting more, striving for success and being ambitious and constantly trying to grow. Some people just want to accept the average and do the minimum. But only dead fish go with the flow. Don't follow that tribe. Create your own tribe. Some people stayed at home and watched 'Saturday Kitchen'. It's not going to get you to the top position in your marketing plan. Use the support networks; relationships equal results. This is about caring. It's not trying to get someone to do something; it's finding out what they want and fulfilling their need. We have to be examples, and I'm not telling everyone to be a supermodel. It's to be an example of what the company inspires. Support your downline, support your upline. What can I do to help you? How can I serve you and show you the way? Of course, I can't do it for you. But if you're hungry and ambitious, I can help you become one of the best success stories in the history of the company."

The most important message from that speech was that of attacking it with unlimited belief: You have to believe 100% that you will be successful. Even when the closest people in your life don't see it or understand it or why you're working so hard.

Remember a farmer doesn't plant a seed on Monday and expect to see a crop on Tuesday. In this business what you do today may show up instantly, but the majority of the time you get to reap the results from the consistent work you did weeks, months and, sometimes years ago.. I will never forget my mum saying to me, "I'm worried about you, you're going to all these meetings and networking events. You're running your gym and then doing more events in the evening. You look exhausted, run down and you've got terrible dark bags under your eyes."

I said, "Mum, these are money bags," as I walked out of the door and rushed off to another event.

Of course, it was tiring, Of course, it was stressful at times. Not everyone sees it or appreciates it, and that's hard. But choose your "hard". It's hard being broke and unfulfilled, too. As long as you see it and understand it, that's all that matters. Keep showing up, keep doing the work. Results will show up. That's law!

Remember, I was in bed with Jim Rohn or Tony Robbins on most nights—usually Jim, as his voice is a bit more relaxing. But Tony is great to wake up with. Seriously, I was constantly feeding my mind with personal development when I could. Falling asleep. Driving to work. Showers. There was no way I was letting negative news or people's opinions (even Mum's) take me off track.

Tracking in your network marketing business comes in the form of knowing your number and making sure you have done the work before you close your eyes each night. How many conversations did I have about my product or business today?

This can be done with a fancy spreadsheet, colored graphics and pop-ups, a flip chart or a note pad and pen. One of my friends told me an even simpler way. He has five coins in his left pocket. When he's had a conversation about his product or business, he moves the coin from the left pocket to the right. He can't go to sleep until he has moved all five coins.

This is tracking in its most simple form, but it works, and you make sure you have the conversations, online, offline or both. Tracking you conversations is vital. Celebrating your "no's" and remembering who to follow up with. Remember the fortune is always in the follow-up.

If you are turned off by tracking, such as when it comes to food, the majority of the world is, replace these thoughts with inspiration by people walking the talk. It is almost a guarantee that they are tracking at least one significant task or transactions of their business, whether it be finances, contacts, goals, conversations, products, speaking engagements…and so on. There is no difference between me and you—just that I've had more no's and slammed doors!

If you're keener to the softer side of your endeavor, realize that you can attack and track becoming a great listener. It's true—you can increasingly test your listening and empathy skills. The content you hear might not be about the business; it might be about someone's life. Focus on the person. Did you start the conversation by asking how you can help?

Did you listen without interruption? Did you freely give feedback and offer to move them along in some way? Did you provide any resources?

I have people come to me all the time clamoring to quit their fulltime businesses as soon as we meet. Process first. Listen to your team's problems and issues. Your business grows by building people. It might take time. (I'm surprised Alex never blocked my number!) Be tenacious. Share. Share the product. Share the opportunity. Share stories. Share resources.

Paying it forward is also a great mentality to have and something Alex always taught me. I think it was naturally in me already, but it was something that network marketing enhanced. I always ask audience members at our conventions to stand up if they bought a ticket for another person to attend. Many do. Conventions don't change your life—your actions thereafter change your life. Purchasing a ticket for someone may have honestly helped to transform someone's life. It's that deep.

I did this for ten people in my team for a leadership convention in Rome. Some of the team members I had only just met, and one had only joined two days before. It was a gamble in many ways but when you offer someone a convention ticket and a hotel room on you, they can't believe the gesture. I always get them to cover their flights, as you need the commitment from them, too.

We are a business and just like any business, you have to invest in it. Our business is people centered so that's where you put your time, energy and money. Not only do they get to see the bigger picture of convention; they also duplicate this with their team the next time a big event comes around. Does it work every time? Like I said, it's a gamble at times. I paid for someone's accommodations and ticket for a convention in Barcelona once and they spent more time at the beach than in the convention. I learned not to invest in that person again. However, out of the ten people that I took to the Rome convention, six of them hit the top leadership positions in the company.

FORTUNE FAVORS THE BRAVE

Our business is like the gym. Some people join and never go; they look at the card in their wallet every day. If you can do better, shouldn't you? Tracking does not have to be sophisticated. Write your goals for the week. Put it on your vision board, your screen saver, on your mirror in thick red lipstick. Cross them out and write them even bigger. Successful people stretch their dreams. Your dreams grow with your cheque, which is just a measuring stick based on the amount of people you have helped.

How many times have you thought of "What if?" or

encouraged someone else to think about it? Illustrating the power of "what if," I use the example of airplanes—people going from one place to another in the sky. People thought of making this happen before it happened. Their legacy lives on through millions of people every single day. Their vision manifests over and over again with the times. In February 2020, British Airways set the record for the quickest flight between New York City and London in just under five hours. Five hours! (It usually takes seven, gate to gate.)

What if you stay up an hour later making phone calls? What if you get up an hour early to walk?

People make the mistake of coming in for the short term without really seeing the bigger life changing potential of this business. This is building a business that will operate month after month. Orchestrate a vision board for six months, a year, five years. Setting and fulfilling goals is addictive. How many doors will a list open?

One of my amazing mentors, Shay O'Brien Senior, (you will hear from his son Shay Junior later) said, "John, this will take you four years of consistent effort, but it will change your life for the better forever. We don't want your money, but to be a success, you will need to invest your time and energy."

That advice took off the pressure to look at the short-term results, gave me a long-term vision and allowed me to trust the process. Shay had been right. I joined in September 2009 and by September 2013, I was making more money in a month from network marketing than I made in a whole year as a personal trainer.

Success leaves clues. I only listen to people who are living the life I want to, or who have had success in the areas I want to succeed. Track your numbers and play the long game and never let impatience get in the way of your master plan.

Repetition is the mother of all skill. Tracking bulletproofs the routine. Reconnect and build a relationship. Build a customer base. Find out who they know. If you bring in thirty-five people, you can fully rely on five to be heavy-hitting players. Don't want to track? How will you know your system is working? How will you know you're speaking to enough people? How will you know you're getting closer? You can't have excuses *and* results. As I have famously said to my fellow Brits, "watching 'East Enders' and 'Coronation Street' four hours a day six days a week equals an extra twenty-four hours, which is a full day."

Is that next boxset binge really going to change your life? I don't even need to answer that one for you!

One of my examples of this replacement is "Today, I will do what others won't, so tomorrow, I can do what others can't," helped me take the whole month of December off one year. I went to New York, Miami, saw my parents and then hit Berlin for New Year's and got paid for the month.

Some people fully live by hardcore principles like this every day.

Again, it's not without pain.

Bethany Hamilton grew up in Hawaii, so it is not surprising to learn that by the age of 7, she was already able to surf waves. In 2003, a terrible tragedy struck when a shark bit off her left arm. As she recovered, she made two promises to herself: The first was that she would not moan about her terrible misfortune and the second was that she would get back on the surfboard. Another person would have been resigned to failure. But not Hamilton. After only 26 days, she was surfing again! She is now ranked as among the top 50 female surfers in the world.

Wheel of Accountability

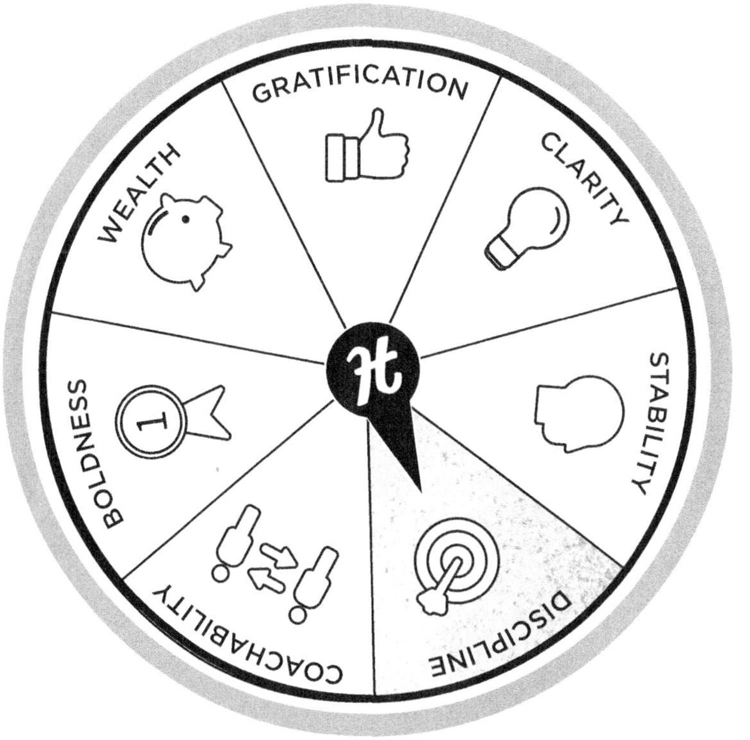

A HIGHER DEGREE OF SELF-CONTROL LEADS TO HAPPINESS.

Don't let impulse dictate your choices.

"The key to successful leadership today is **influence**, not authority."

—KEN BLANCHARD

CHAPTER 6

MENTORS—

WHO'S WHO?

IS THAT YOU?

Searching for Your Truth

How often do you use social media to share something purely beneficial to others?

Are you coachable?

Do you equally talk and execute?

Do you practice communicating by presenting to a small group or speaking in public?

Alex Hamer-Webb, one of the most incredible individuals I've ever known, was my mentor for just under ten years before he passed away in July 2019. Alex had been with our company for just over twenty-seven years and played a pivotal part of the success with our company, especially with our UK business. In 2013, when Generation Y and social media swept across Europe, he had the ability and foresight to embrace change and helped thousands of people improve their lives for the better with the team Rhino movement and later, with the team Heart movement.

It was a time in our business we will all look back on with immense pride. You had to be part of it to really get it. I remember we had that much excitement and fun that people were just attracted to our energy. We filled hotel convention centers at the drop of a flyer to promote an event, breaking fire regulations and causing hysteria in every venue we went to.

We were on a mission. We had finally found a way to change our lives and we wanted to tell the world. Of course, we made mistakes, but our intentions were always true. From superhero fancy dress parties at conventions to boat trips around Majorca and Marbella, to simple personal development festivals in a field with tepees and campfires, one thing we did know how to do was create a vibe like no one else that was open to everyone and totally inclusive.

Everyone was welcome. Everyone had a home and a place in our crew. There was never any judgement— just a smile, a handshake and a hug.

I remember being in an Irish bar in Barcelona after a convention with Alex, Rob and a couple of other team members. The bar was empty, and we were watching the football. I uploaded a picture of us on Facebook and tagged us in the Irish bar. Within forty-five minutes, about 200 people had flooded in and another 150 packed the bar across the street. A few hours later, we had taken over the whole square. It was crazy. The bar still remembers us for that day. I think it's the best Sunday they've ever had in terms of profit!

But that was what we did. I remember Alex saying, "You don't learn this business. You feel it." It was a simple philosophy of, if I'm nice to you, then you will be nice to me, and if I welcome you, then you will welcome another. As Jesus said, "Treat people how you want to be treated."

It's no coincidence that when you build your business with this mentality of helping others, magic happens. You will have growth in every area you touch.

Alex would talk about his old days and described himself as a Rastafarian hairdresser with long dreadlocks and torn jeans. He was a rock star and didn't apologize for it. He didn't want to be judged for what he wore or who he was, as he was true to himself and would always compliment other people on their own individual style and authenticity. Because he didn't want to be judged, he never judged others. I could write a whole book on what he taught me and literally thousands of other people and another book on the crazy fun stories we created over the years.

At one of the first conventions I attended, we crashed a wedding that was going on in the next room. We stayed for about forty minutes dancing with the bride and groom and chatting with the family members. Two of us were "work colleagues" and Alex was "the uncle who had flown in from Jamaica". It was hilarious, harmless fun and getting to know other people.

What made Alex such an outstanding mentor, and what I have tried to emulate, is that he was always very passionate, positive and persuasive about helping his team move forward, both on personal and business levels. Alex's sweeping statement he would want to leave us with was, "The future is so bright, we all need to wear sunglasses." I still tear up, hearing him say this in his radio-like voice.

Like everyone, Alex had a back story as a part of his evolution. He was brought up in children's homes from the age of 2 to 15, was dyslexic, never had any direction, and then became a hairdresser for twenty-five years. He enjoyed what he did, but as he famously said in many interviews, his future looked like he would end up as an old barber if he didn't make some changes.

Someone had approached Alex about this business, and he borrowed a suit to "show up" to a convention with 2,000 people. He worked so hard, that when he entered this business, Alex didn't care if anyone said "yes." He said he "failed his way" to his status as a millionaire, touching thousands in our organization. "Money is a byproduct for helping others achieve what they want in life," Alex said. "Believe in yourself, believe in your dreams, and don't let anyone stop you in what you want to do in life."

Our business is going through a monstrous growth surge, using the philosophy he taught us, combined with the power and speed of online technology. He certainly has created a legacy that lives on and continues to impact many lives.

Writing for *Inc.* magazine, Jayson Demers, founder and CEO of Audiencebloom, outlined seven key qualities of an effective mentor:

1. **Ability and willingness to communicate what you know.** Being clear when you communicate the lessons you've learned, or the strategies or guidance you're offering, is essential, as is your level of desire to communicate the intricate details in a way that makes sense and that your mentee can understand and learn from.

2. **Preparedness.** Being a mentor means making an important, serious commitment to someone, so give your mentee—and the process—the respect he or she deserves. Show your faith in your mentee's abilities and in the process by preparing for each mentoring session.

3. **Approachability, availability, and the ability to listen.** Your mentee must feel comfortable approaching you for advice or consultation; however, he or she must keep your availability and your schedule in mind.

4. **Honesty with diplomacy.** Any questions that aren't addressed can lead to concerns and problems, so you owe it to your mentee to be candid and straightforward. Say what you think your mentee *needs* to hear from you, not what you think he or she might *want* to hear.

5. **Inquisitiveness.** Mentors continue learning about what's going on in your industry or business, your school, your community, or the world at large.

6. **Objectivity and fairness.** Ensure that there's no hidden agenda or ulterior motives involved in this relationship.

7. **Compassion and genuineness.** Compassion motivates people to go out of their way to help the physical, mental, or emotional pains of another and themselves.

ALWAYS COACHABLE, NEVER COCKY

Now you know what you should be looking for in a mentor, and I'm sorry that Alex Hamer-Webb couldn't mentor the entire planet! But it's not just about the mentor. They say when the student is ready, the teacher arrives. What does being "coachable" look like in mentality and behavior?

The one thing we can't teach is hunger. I ask people what they want out of this business and what they're willing to do. If their expectations do not match their work ethic, there is the first red flag. I always give people early challenges to gauge their hunger. If I assign an audio book to listen to and someone does it straight away, I know they are teachable. I get them to write their prospect list and do a launch post on social media. The quicker they do it the more hungry they are. When I first met my mentor, I learned to follow his blueprint and then add my own personality. The key building blocks are the same, but you develop your own system. Be open to discuss ideas. The concepts have remained the same over the years, but the tools have changed. Back in the 90s, it was three calls, in-home meetings and hotel conference room meetings. When I started out, you handed out DVDs and brochures. There was no Instagram, no Facebook live, no Zoom or WhatsApp.

Even though we evolved into a social media business, the 2020 quarantine has shown us how it easy it is with technology to make communication so much easier. To share stories and build culture across the globe with the click of a button. Remember though, your job remains the same. Share your product and your story. Share your opportunity and teach others to do the same thing. Technology is on your side. But you need to communicate with people effectively. Be a nice human and want to help people win!

In our business, it has to be duplicable. Sometimes you get massive ego-driven people, who try to change the business altogether. Simplicity adds speed. We want to be able to teach it and then have others teach it.

My No. 1 direction to the team is, "Tell me when you've done it!" Not all the chatter leading up to not doing it. I can help you get something better or right. I respond to deserve, *not need*, and done, *not doing*.

I see so many people get inspired from an event or call and the next thing they do is tell the social media world, "Here's what is coming" or "watch this space" or "I mean business this time". You don't need to tell the world what you're going to do. Just get on with it. Attack it and track it and celebrate when it's done. There is nothing more inspiring than leading from the front with actions, not just words.

As we are all strung together by an hour-long call or Zoom meeting in which you, as leader, need to bring a listening ear, energy, an inspiring message, organization, results, and clear objectives, roles and responsibilities cannot be compromised by the "casualness" of virtual business. In fact, I would argue that they are even more essential, given the looser nature of this communication exchange. For instance, you don't know each other's operating environment or what else may be going on in that room, distracting them. Also, since you don't see body language and other communication cues in how your team members are receiving your information, you really need to turn up your energy.

Have communication tools strengthened our business and the way we operate? Entirely. However, there is a trap door you need to avoid, which is losing the true power of human connection. This is why I prefer Zoom to Facebook for online events, simply because you can see your team, and they can see you.

I will also never abandon live events because the love and connection are elevated massively when you get together with people face to face. The stories always seem more real and more inspiring when you're all in the same room. The laughter is infections and the tears, contagious, as you hear real stories from normal people who are showing you the path to walk towards your hopes and dreams.

The live events and togetherness are the glue that keeps the team connected when times get tough. There have been some very tough times over the years where the friendships built at the events have kept us all together and in it as one team. My direct upline, Rob, and I, had so much fun in the early days. We loved traveling around the UK doing events and meeting new people. As the business and success intensified, the traveling did, and we found ourselves in some amazing cities around Europe and America.

During quarantine from the coronavirus, I ran power hours online with between 600 and 1,500 people logging in from all over the world. These numbers would be impossible on a weekly basis without reliable communication. If nothing else did, a pandemic showed us that we have to keep business going.

TEAM FORMATION AND FIREWORKS

One of the most common stories I hear is how leaders see

the potential in their team, but the team doesn't quite share the same belief. They can't understand why it feels like an uphill battle to get the collective results, why targets are getting missed, and it's just not coming together. You and your team should be flying along, but in reality, you're not.

One thing I live by and look for in others as you have probably noticed throughout this book is evidence of ACTIONS speaking louder than words. You're dealing with people—people have emotions and allow distractions to creep in. One day, they're highly motivated and inspired to work on their dreams; the next day, the energy is flat because of an argument with their partner, a big fat no, an order that got canceled or a night out that never ended.

It so important that you have key structured building blocks in place, and you have safety in numbers. So, if one teamie is off track, you have another to put your energy into. It's also vital that you have something to plug people into as quickly as possible. The longer they stay off track or wallow in that self-pity, the harder it is to get them to show up.

If leading your team is a challenge, exhausting, frustrating or just excruciating sometimes, then learn how to make it so much easier.

The ability to be an empowered leader is as vital as water, food and oxygen. We don't get incredible results by just turning up. We get results when leaders show up, give clear direction, take action, share the knowledge, spend time cultivating a winning culture and consistently doing the work. The guiding force is to always be striving toward innovative ways to:

- Create a great team with a winning culture comprised of "big actions"

- Get your entire team working in collaboration, pulling in the same direction so you can grow and thrive together

- Consistently engage with your team to keep motivation and enthusiasm an ongoing theme

- Maximize the return of capabilities; knowledge is power, and you will know how to keep your team involved and leverage their skills across the whole team

- Develop a caring nurturing environment to allow your team to share their challenges so the whole team can grow and learn from the experience

- Focus the team energy to outward competition, getting you all over the line as a team
- Create a way to open up powerful discussions that the whole team benefit from, but taking the reins with final decisions
- Communicate your ideas, encourage collaboration and build a team of like-minded leaders
- Create stronger relationships
- Celebrate the small wins; big wins are just the small ones added up
- Strive to create leaders, not followers
- Remember the 80/20 rule or the 80/15/4/1 law, as I've now defined it to be: 80% of your team just want to be part of something and earn a bit. They are happy with up to $1,000 per month in income; 15% want to earn above $1000-$5000; 4% want to become six-figure earners; 1% want to become seven-figure earners and above.

Our job is to find what people want and help them get it. Put your time and energy into the people that deserve it and want to grow the most. Train the 80% on mass and the core 20% upper-level leadership should be getting your high-quality time and energy. As Shay would always say to me, "Work with the workers."

In my experience, key to any relationship in this business is the ability to motivate—yourself and others…consistently. Motivation is a wonderful gift from mentors near and far. In fact, you can have role models and mentors that you never meet. As long as these figures emit something that you would like to mirror, continue looking to them.

For example, thought of by some as one of the best boxers in the world, Manny Pacquiao's life wasn't always smooth sailing. He was born in the Philippines, lived in a shack with a dirt floor, and scrapped for food when he had to. As a child, Manny would help out his family by selling bread on busy city streets. At just age 16, Pacquiao discovered his true gift for fighting, often in times of self-defense. Pacquiao went on to become a professional boxer, is the only eight-division world champion, and has won 11 major world titles. He's won titles in four weight classes: welterweight, lightweight, featherweight, and flyweight. As if his professional boxing, a rags to riches story wasn't enough to make history, Pacquiao went on to become a politician (serving as a Senator) in the

Philippines. His story is truly one that is motivational!

Wheel of Accountability

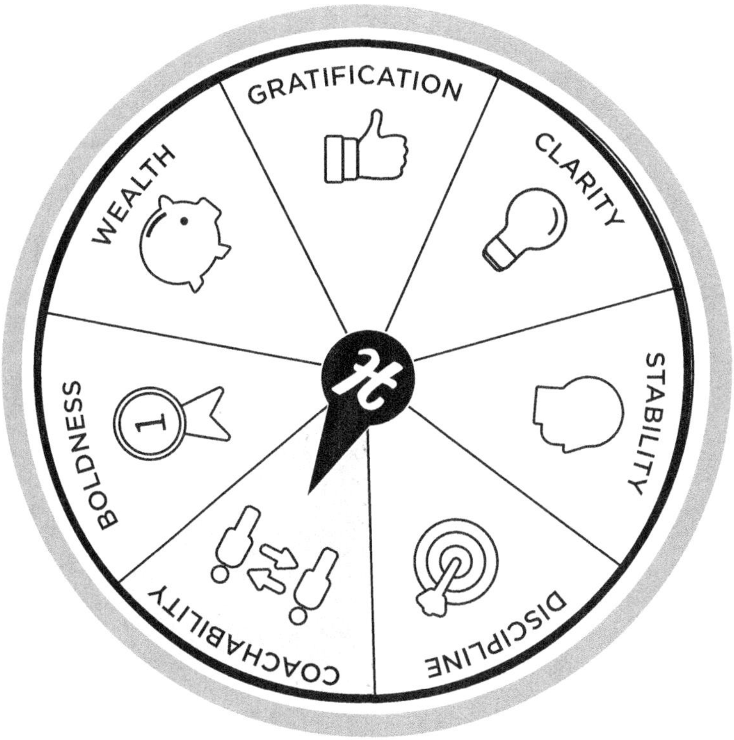

TAKE 15 MINUTES TO LEARN SOMETHING NEW EVERY DAY.

"Comfort zones are plush-lined coffins. When you stay in your plush-lined coffins, **you die.**"

—STAN DALE

CHAPTER 7

GRATITUDE AND AMBITION OF THE TITANS

Searching for Your Truth

Who do you look up to? Why?

When was the last time you couldn't afford something you really wanted?

Which ability would be most transformative for you to improve?

Do you know your top five values in life?

Feeling content, secure and in control? You may be languishing in your comfort zone—complete with a memory foam pillow, milk, and cookies (or tea and cake, depending on your fancy)! I know when I travel, I always look forward to the hotel perks and turn-down service. I confess, that is a comfort zone that is hard for me to leave sometimes.

Boxing champion Marvin Hagler said, "It's real hard to get up at 5:00 a.m. and run five miles when you're in a four-poster bed wearing silk pajamas."

But ultimately, what allures outside the door is far more satisfying—possibilities. Possibilities are the difference between fear and fortune. Possibilities can wake you up out of the most peaceful sleep when you are driven.

What is your comfort zone? What are ways you've gone outside of it? In truth, a comfort zone is something to be grateful for. Comfort is not a bad thing when you think of the opposite of comfort being *uncertainty*. But we need to get to the heart of the definition when it comes to living life on your own terms. The zone of comfort keeps you still, stuck, yearning rather than obtaining. The questions presented at the beginning of this chapter are meant to stir your ambitions. For example, the person you look up to may possess a trait, asset, or lifestyle you don't have but aspire to.

There is a fine line between gratitude and ambition.

You're grateful for what you have but maintain ambition to get better. Jim Rohn said, "If you could do more, should you?" We're in a service business, serving other people. That comfort zone is saying it's hard to stay hungry when you can go to bed in silk pajamas every night! Especially in the Western world, it's easy to stay in and glue yourself to Netflix or scroll and roll through Instagram all day. Three hours can go by in a flash.

What kind of life is waiting for you outside your comfort zone? That waitress that gave impeccable service would be incredible at your business but you didn't have the courage to break free of your comfort zone and say, "Hey, I know you're super busy, but I just wanted to say you were outstanding at your job today. I think you would be incredible at what I do and I'm looking for people exactly like you. Can I message you on Instagram later on and share with you what I do?" It's that simple. But it takes courage.

Another angle is, if you want to be a top earner, you need to get out of your comfort zone. I do public speaking now in front of thousands. There is no way I would have done that when I first started. I was in a seminar and they asked for a volunteer. I forced myself. I never did anything like that before. I got out of my comfort zone. It was my first real moment of thinking, *screw it! What is the worst that can happen?*

People build stories of fear and resistance in their mind. *What if I say something stupid? What if I stammer? What if I fall in these heels?* And it all happens, believe me. I've either seen it or experienced it myself. Well, with practice, you get better and better. And what if you replaced that fear mindset with a fortune mindset? There is almost always a positive thought you can muster in any given situation. If you can't think of one at the time relatively quickly, try embedding terms like *growth*, *learning*, *experience*.

In the public speaking arena, I kept putting myself forward. Even in my fitness business, I had never run a boot camp. I had never taught a class. But when I set up my studio and advertised my first class, I knew eventually, I would have to teach a session. The most I had ever trained before were two or three people. The truth is, your audience only knows what you tell them and what you show them. I was honest. "Welcome to the very first bootcamp in the new studio. I'm sure it won't go 100% to plan, but I can promise you fun and hard work and you will walk out of here feeling better than when you arrived."

The fear of doing it and the story you tell yourself is never as bad as actually doing it. The elation injection you get when it's over, the sense of accomplishment and pride for pushing yourself and conquering your fear, is pure bliss!

We say in our industry, "The person with the marker makes the money." This means that they were in the front of the room with a marker, directing others and engaging with the audience. They are leading the room. They are influencing. They are the ones presenting. They are the ones doing the Facebook live then onto running the Zoom call. They project authority.

Are you doing enough Facebook lives? Or is something holding you back? What's the story you keep telling yourself? That you will get negative comments. Nobody will watch it. You'll say something stupid. The truth is it very rarely happens, and if it does, make a joke about it and move on to the next moment.

I remember running a bootcamp once and nobody showed up! I did a workout myself, took a picture of me in a pool of sweat next to the kettlebells and dumbbells and posted it on my socials. I wrote, "Great bootcamp tonight, thanks to everyone who showed up. See you tomorrow for more of the same." Guess what? The next day, the class was full! Stay in the lane and keep moving forward, finding the positive in every opportunity.

The next time you're luxuriating in your comfort zone, or even tossing and turning in your comfort zone as a result of that gut instinct that something should be different, it's the choice of two pains—doing what you didn't want to do, or the pain of sticking with your current situation and turning down a scary but tantalizing opportunity or telling your kids that you can't afford Christmas or a vacation this year.

Need some inspirational examples of the level of things you may be able achieve if you leave your comfort zone?

Quebec native Marie-France Roy began snowboarding at age 11. After years spent honing her skills on Mount Éboulements in Canada, Roy solidified herself as a "legend" when she made her X Games debut as a freestyle snowboarder. Roy has racked up the medals and the sponsorships. She's a face for Red Bull and Patagonia.

Xavier De Le Rue is a big mountain snowboarder hailing from France. Xavier began his pro career on the Boardercross pro tour, and since then, has taken home myriad medals and titles, including two gold medals from the FIS Snowboarding World Championships. Xavier has been named "big mountain rider of the year" by *Snowboarder* magazine.

Horacio Llorens can credit his early start in paragliding to his uncle, who owns a paragliding school in Llorens's native Spain. He began his professional career in 2000. In 2012, he jumped from a helicopter at 19,700 feet above Guatemala and broke a world record with 568 consecutive loops. A few years later, he jumped from a plane in Tromso, Norway to experience night flying amongst the Aurora Borealis. He has won just about every major competition for both sincro and solo gliding. Llorens took gold at the World Air Games and has won the world championships five times.

Wheel of Accountability

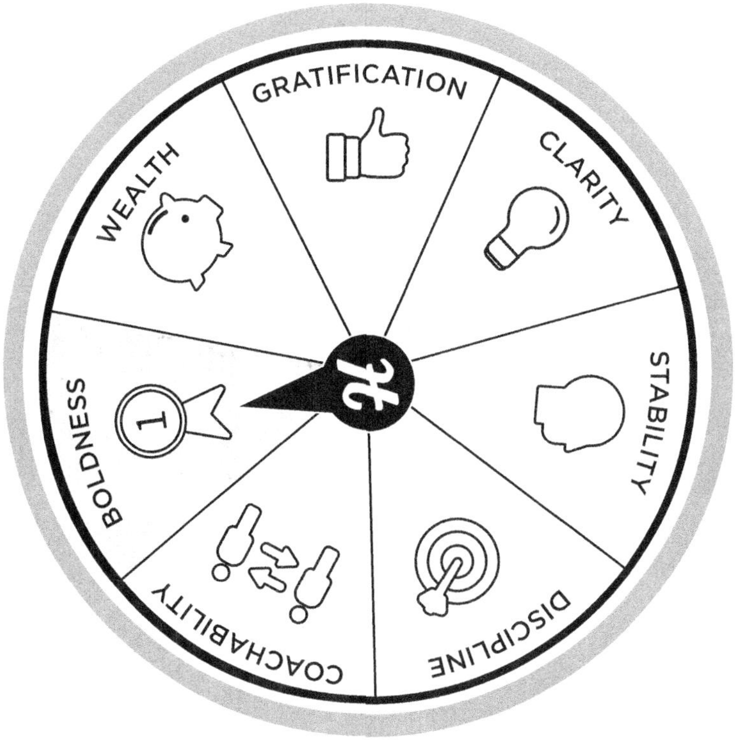

CLOSE UP YOUR COMFORT ZONES AND OPEN THE DOOR TO GREATNESS.

Small changes add up!

"A great mind becomes a great fortune."

—SENECA

CHAPTER 8

LITERACY IN FORTUNES

Searching for Your Truth

Do you check negative internal messages or let them send you into a tailspin?

Do you maintain a budget?

How many hours a week might you spend watching TV?

What does financial freedom represent for you next year? In five years?

Money management is a massive topic. In the traditional sense, it spans budgeting, banking and saving, paying taxes, investing, managing debt, retirement planning, and estate planning. However, as money relates to network marketing and living life on your own terms, I want to talk about financial responsibility as an entrepreneur, making money work for you, sustaining your business, and reinvesting. The other tasks relating to money are too individual to tackle here. There are personal finance apps galore these days. This information you will not find in that tiny frame painting the picture of your incoming and outgoing currency.

We'll center on being a good custodian of money. I will go ahead and say it, and I'm sorry if this does not sound romantic: Making a lot of money upfront has two negative effects on those who hit it hard out the gate and then crash and burn extraordinarily quick: They take their foot off the gas, so they stop doing what it took in the first place when in reality, they should be focused on sustaining success. They've hit a comfort zone and hung their hat on the money they've earned.

Let's face it and be totally honest here. You joined your business to make some financial benefit. Now, I'm not obsessed with money and I don't actually need a lot of it to have a simple and gratifying life. However, I joined my business for a financial benefit. It started for me with a goal of finding a way to wipe out the bills that stressed me out each month. I then did an exercise called "live for free" where my sole aim was to be able to live from my network marking income. It would cover my outgoings, replacing my full-time income and giving me money to enjoy life. As my business started to grow and I began to make more income and tick things off on the vision board, temptations and flashing lights started to appear.

I've mentioned this earlier, but it's okay to let fear motivate you a little and that's what I did. I saved, invested and committed to looking after my income. I listened to others that had built wealth, reading the books and watching the YouTube clips. The reason being, I was scared of being that guy who blew it all or the person that made it, lost it and ended up back where they started. You hear these horror stories all the time—especially in the sporting and entertainment arena. Don't get me wrong. I splashed out on a few nice things for myself and for people I care about but I'm not really into designer clothes, I'm more into designer experiences, so a lot of my income in the early days was put into doing some cool trips abroad.

Just be careful you don't fall into the trap of buying stuff you don't really need or even want. Don't get too eager to spend it because it's there. I've seen people blow money on clothes, cars, first-class tickets everywhere, and share the lifestyle images because they feel like this will draw others to the business. Of course, it can have some positive impact and it will motivate or inspire your team, and I honestly feel you have to go there a little if that urge is in you. If it's always been your dream to splash out a little, just have some boundaries. Know that it can actually turn people off. Maybe they feel you're boasting, or they see what you're doing as a grandiose stretch for them.

Someone said to me once, "I don't know how you do what you do, all those flights and hotels. Never being at home." I was posting on my socials thinking it would inspire, but it actually created a lot of watchers and envious admirers than people saying, "I can do that, and I want to join his team."

People don't join our business to buy a private jet. They join our business to pay for the kids' school fees, take an extra vacation a year, spend more time at home, and maybe buy the car of their dreams.

One other thing I've seen with living life this way is unnecessary financial pressure people put on themselves by unnecessary spending. They joined to create financial stress-free living, but the choices they made caught up with them to cause more financial stress than they had before they joined. Don't get me wrong; you always grow again and recover, but do you really want to make that mistake in the first place?

The best investment you can make is always into yourself,

your team and your business. I've spent thousands on convention tickets for my team over the years. I've spent thousands on retreats and success trips. I've spent thousands on champagne, too (with lots of promotions to celebrate over the years). Most importantly, I've spent thousands on personal development in order to grow my mindset and my personal brand.

I love the Jim Rohn quote, "When do you buy the second car? When you have bought the second house."

Finance guru Suze Orman said, "You're never powerful in life until you're powerful over your own money." She has 25 million copies of books in circulation, so perhaps listen to her. And what makes her real is the fact that she wanted to be a waitress when she grew up and then open up a restaurant, which was funded by $50,000 in checks and promissory notes by faithful customers who wanted to encourage her dream! They said she had ten years to pay this money off, if she could, without interest. It's safe to say Orman's life took many turns thereafter, and today, she is one of the most respected finance educators in the world. But what's evident is that she was shown the most amazing example of the power of people believing in you and your dream. As you make some money, blow some money, and invest some, don't forget about your actions and how they may influence others.

If the goal is financial independence, why earn loads of

money and then create more problems and financial stress? If you legitimately have money to burn, there is nothing wrong with enjoying all it affords you. Simultaneously, invest the money into your team or marketing tools. Invest money into your body and your brain—personal development.

Examples of these investments are:

- Communication and collaboration tools for virtual working; upgrades to your phone, computer, video platforms like Zoom and Cisco WebX

- Lighting or décor for the environment you're conducting video meetings on (I see this need a lot!)

- Professional memberships that are educational in nature and/or lead to greater leads

- Conferences and continuing education

- Fitness clothes and equipment

- Nutrition plans or systems (JuicePlus is an obvious one!)

- Skincare
- Transportation (I'm going to leave this open-ended because it's so arbitrary; all things cars, trains, planes!)
- Private meeting space for business travel (this could mean an upgrade at a hotel or reservation at a co-working space, like WeWork or Regus, which have worldwide locations and allow access 24/7)
- Business lunches or dinners for your best prospects and teams
- Recreational retreats—we all need a break outside of our homes and hometowns

Need an extreme example of investing in your personal development? NBA "King" LaBron James spends up to $1.5 million a year on his massage therapist, a cryo chamber, hyperbaric chamber, compression gear, home gyms, chefs, appliances, all the tools that help his performance.

Wheel of Accountability

WEALTH, IN WHATEVER FORM, IS A RESULT BASED ON ACTIONS.

Act don't just talk or think.

PART 2.

SUCCESS TRIBE

"Start from **wherever** you are and with **whatever** you've got."

—JIM ROHN

CHAPTER 9

FRESH STARTS

Features of Fortune

- Courage
- Determination
- Discipline
- Community
- Decisiveness
- Ambition
- Adventure

In network marketing and living life on your own terms, fresh starts abound. I never get tired of sharing stories of them. As of this writing in summer 2020, I guarantee you that fresh starts far exceed old paradigms, professions, and ways of working no matter who you ask or where you turn. Here are just a few favorites involving a select diverse group of individuals I have gotten to know over the years. I will stress that their stories are raw and uncut because that is how we do in this business—if little editing of the content is the difference between inspiring one reader, it will have been worth including them as a positive portrayal of what is possible.

RECKONING AND RESILIENCE:
PAULA MCGUIRE, MANCHESTER, ENGLAND

Q: What is the most recent goal you achieved by living life on your own terms?

A: My partner and I bought a house two months ago. We're living together for the first time and have six girls between us and a granddaughter. We have three of them here, so there is a lot of activity here during lockdown.

Q. We want people to know they have options. Can you start with your background and outlook now?

A. I have always been self-employed with an entrepreneurial mindset in traditional business. My main previous business was in elderly care, providing careers for people who were living in their homes, elderly and disabled, working alongside social services where they're coordinating care packages and meals. It was very stressful working with vulnerable people. Obviously, the job had to be done right. My parents were both entrepreneurial and brought me up to think I could live the life I wanted if I worked hard. In fact, when I was 10, in 1976, totally unheard of, my parents got a little British motor home and brought it over to America on our boat and traveled around the States for 12 months. British people didn't do this kind of thing! This was my example from parents. I was always striving for more. I got married, had three daughters, was the breadwinner and had a difficult marriage.

We renovated a lot of property, so we didn't

struggle for money. But what I never had was time-freedom. I could never leave it for very long. If I did, I came back to a lot of problems. Even though I had financial success over 20 years, I became ill with the stress of the business and my marriage breaking down. It was a really tough time and I amassed horrible debt. Things were not great for a number of years. In 2010, I walked away from the business and marriage.

My parents have a place in Palm Springs. They stay there January through April. They came back this year earlier because of the coronavirus. In 2012, they were there, and a lady introduced my mom to JuicePlus. They took it and felt better. I was still dealing with a lot of health stuff. My mom sent me the products. I literally took it because she told me. I had no clue about the product or networking marketing. She invited me to a "little meeting" with John, who had just been in the business a couple of years. I would have been a young teenage mom to him! Or a big sister. We got on so well, I thought I would like to work with this man. We hit it off. The more meetings I went to, the more positive energy of this I craved. Particularly in contrast to my former business. It radiated out of John. He is magnetic. People flock to him. He was wise beyond his years even then. Between my vision and his vision, I could see that I could live that life, too.

Q. What was the vision?

A. Both financial and time freedom. I lived in a nice house, was free from my ex-husband but what I did have was the debt. It took me several years to get rid of that debt. I could see more time and living life on my terms. I like to do several things with my day, and I love people, not sitting behind a desk for eight hours a day. The idea of traveling and working with John and all these people with great energy, wow, it was so tempting. We were like the blind leading the blind back then. We knew how to have fun and share the product but didn't really know the marketing plan or know how to read reports. Everybody helped each other. Our organization links arms and pulls and drags each other around and up to success. There was always someone to ask. That really appealed to me. About three or four years in, I managed to get myself debt-free. It's been instrumental in getting me physically and mentally well and progressing through life.

Q: What were you drawn to most about the business?

A. Our sense of community is truly like a family. I've been eight years with our business, so I've seen many people come and go. If someone comes with the wrong attitude or just money signs in their eyes, they don't last long. It really is about helping people and feeling the responsibility to help people. That is my yellow nature, my responsibility to help people. John is like that as well. He needs a lot of fun, but he will go above and beyond to help somebody.

Q. If you look at the whole infrastructure of this business and who you mentor, what are your

tips? What things do you focus on? I know you emphasize a larger purpose holding it together for them.

A. The money made is only a reflection of the people you are helping. There is so much more to it. A phrase: "As long as you are helping enough people in life, you will always get what you want." It's about helping people achieve their goals. We gather no's but they're not saying no to you, they need to see the vision. It's challenging right now, and people are struggling, not knowing if they will have a job or where income will go. We need to let them know there is a plan B, likewise with our products. Our company is incredible. It's about having belief in yourself to pass on that information to other people. My main drive at the moment is telling people they have options. It's about speaking to enough people. What I have never lost is my total passion for this. I'm always hopeful the next person I speak to will help me achieve my dreams. People I tend to speak to are my age. John's demographics are younger. If I had known about this business when my kids were younger, I would have joined. My kid was one when it was created! I just didn't know about it.

Q. How do you deal with fear and self-doubt?

A. There will always be fear and self-doubt, but it's what you do with it. Even the most confident or secure person deals with this. That goes hand in hand with self-development, which is a huge part of our business. You're naturally growing as a person with our conventions and how we work as teams, but we're really advocates of self-development. I once tried to do self-development when I was married to my ex-husband. He really wouldn't entertain anything like that; very much a control freak, so I couldn't go down that route. As soon as this business came along and people were talking about *The Secret* and Laws of Attraction, I caught onto that like wildfire. I work this every day and I love it. I don't think you can stop working on yourself. With any new teammate, if I'm doing a presentation, I will always tell people to tap into the resources for self-development because it helps when that self-doubt creeps in. You need to be able to deal with no and not take it personally. They're saying no to themselves. You can only get that straight with your mind if you've worked on your mindset.

Last night, on Zoom, they brought in a life coach to talk about mindset for forty-five minutes. It was fantastic. It's amazing that so many people don't know of self-development. It doesn't matter what business you're in or the situation at hand. We can all become better people by tapping into these resources and developing our minds. Better businesspeople but better in every relationship we've got!

TOTAL TRANSFORMATION: EMMA CAREN WILSON, FLEET, HAMPSHIRE, ENGLAND

Q. How has it been working with a mentor?

A. John has been an amazing mentor. He just started helping my husband. He's really approachable.

He's extremely successful and one of the best entrepreneurs I know. He always does what he says he will do. He always shows up and puts others before himself. The five people you spend the most time with is are the ones your life will mirror. Hard worker but so much fun. There is not a bad bone in his body. I just think he's an amazing person.

Q. What behaviors and routines have you developed as an entrepreneur?

A. Self-development is part of my daily life. Gratitude has been a massive part of our journey and attracting success. I've learned to work from home with lots of distractions. In the beginning, I was doubtful about how much success I would have. I had to borrow 50 pounds from my mother because I didn't have the money to join the business. Because I borrowed it, I was more driven to be successful. I used to be fearful of speaking in public. I needed to be hypnotized before I spoke in front of seven people—I used to cry my way through all of the presentations, but I think that was more about my situation of being a single mom and how much pain that brought me. There is a phrase: "Do it anyway." Always say yes and drive yourself forward. Push through. You cry less and less!

In 2012, when I was going to give my business upin between two promotions because I thought I couldn't do this anymore, John said one day, "There will be one person on stage who's made a million pounds, and you'll wish that were you." I stayed in because there is always a fear of missing out."

Q. Through the evolution of your business, what is an example of a sacrifice you made for your self-development?

A. In the first two and a half years of the business, I didn't do anything else but maybe celebrate birthdays. My mentality was first and last thing at night toward my business and nothing else. I would get up and do training in the morning. My daughter was at nursery, so I did put her in childcare so I could focus more. I would do an event until 11:00 at night, then drive up to Liverpool to my mother's where my daughter may be. Get up at 3:00 in the morning. Then another event the next day. We lived, breathed, worked. New Year's Eve, 2013, I was at Disney Land with one of my team members, trying to reconfigure positions on a mini-holiday. It didn't feel like work. It felt like life. That is how we created such success. The more success you have, the more success your team has. It's a success circle.

I had a three-and-a-half-month baby at the time I joined JuicePlus, and I set out to make money part-time. Single mom, no money and really struggling. My parents were helping me. Before this, I was in uni and working in a mental health unit. I was 24 years old, but I'm quite a driven person so I was really lucky to stumble on networking marketing to have an income around my daughter.

John has been rather motivational in life. He was a great person to be around with great energy. When I got my second promotion, he asked me to be a qualifying national marketing director. From day one, he's been a great team leader. He makes the best out of any situation. Positivity. As our business has progressed, watching him and leading from the front. We call him "Team Rhino Jesus!" He's a dear friend of mine, came to my wedding and is part of my family, but I will always look up to him as a leader and entrepreneur.

A phrase we used to say is, "'F' everything and run it anyway." No matter what happens, carry on. We've lived by what if. The what-ifs have always paid off. Our business is only 50 pounds as the investment, so it's not a big risk up front, but it has paid off so massively. Risk always pays off.

DRIVEN BY HEALTH AND HOPE: CARLY PEACE, LIVERPOOL, ENGLAND

Q. How did you get started in network marketing?

A. I met John in 2013 at my first ever event. It was in a small cricket club, I nearly talked myself out of going in and it's the best thing I ever did; cheesy but that night changed my life! John came over to introduce himself at the end of the event and I took an instant liking to him, he was just so welcoming, friendly and approachable. Since then, he's been my strongest arm to reach out for in my business. I know he will answer all of my questions and be there for support. He's the most inspirational man I know! Very blessed and grateful to have him as a mentor, he's the kind of person that makes you feel motivated just by being in his presence. Every conversation or time with John I leave feeling full of life and like I can achieve anything.

I was attracted to the thought of having a little more from life. I loved the community it brought me straight away, something new and exciting to chase every day that give me a new exciting purpose right from the beginning! I was a young mum still living at home with my mum, no savings, doing a job I disliked, worried and uncertain about the future. This gave me back hope and excitement that I could actually achieve things I had wanted to even whilst looking after my boy. I also wanted to be a personal trainer and so the business worked fab hand in hand with supporting others toward a healthy lifestyle.

Q. What was your signature sacrifice during this time?

A. I don't feel it was so much a sacrifice. I just made the business a priority through sheer passion and determination. I loved climbing the bonus system, I felt alive, happy and purpose driven again. It's funny because I joined for extra money but then I didn't feel like I was chasing that; I was chasing the good feels of the whole business and the money seemed to follow the more I drove to help more people. As they say, "Help as many people get what they want, and you'll get everything you want." I stopped watching TV, didn't go on as many social events for the first year, and saved my bonuses to really make an impact on my life. I bought my house in cash.

Q. What are your tips for increasing your confidence?

A. I feel like I'm just someone who will never give up no matter how hard things get. When I have a personal goal, I am now relentless until I reach it. I help people get their goals and I hit mine. I love the personal growth and the self-development and goal setting the business brought me, as every day, I wake up now striving to be the best and get the best from my day and that's because of the mindset the business has given to me. I love being creative, trying new things, and helping others get their success. It's addictive.

Fear and self-doubt, I have had a lot of and definitely still do at times. I don't enjoy speaking in public. On large calls, I worry whether people think I'm not good enough or judge me. But what's worse? Overcoming these things or not doing them and not having the lifestyle the business has given to me and my family. Feel the fear and do it anyway—you always feel proud after overcoming these fears and challenges.

MOM ON A MISSION: SINAED KAVANAGH

Q. What appealed to you about network marketing? What was your former career or circumstance?

A. Before network marketing, I was in corporate sales and always loved how competitive it was and the idea of having a commission-structured pay. Even back then, it was exciting knowing my income was directly related to the effort I put in, but I was still limited by what I was able to produce in a day. Then network marketing came along. I remember when I first learned of network marketing—with its unlimited earnings, working from anywhere, being part of a team where people celebrate you and want to see you win...it seemed too good to be true. What I've experienced over the years is that it's actually much, much more. Being in this industry has changed my life in more ways than I could ever have imagined. I'm surrounded by positive people every day who aren't afraid to work for their dreams. It's really given me a purpose, and it has pushed me to want to show my daughter she can have anything she's willing to work for.

Q. What are the keys to your success, and do you have the same advice for others who need their Plan B in current times?

A. I believe the key to success is deciding exactly what you want, and then committing to do whatever you need to do to get it. You have to be brave enough to start, and then resilient enough to keep going even when it gets tough. The thing about success is that it looks different to all of us. Many of us are brought up with ideals on what success should be like (a stable job, etc.) but that way of living and working doesn't really exist anymore. These companies and industries aren't as solid as we were led to believe. Having a plan B is really having a plan A and creating a life that feels just as good as you want it to look.

Q. What behaviors/routines have you adopted as a successful entrepreneur? How do you manage fear and self-doubt?

A. I used to have the worst routine when it came to building my business because I was just so excited for it, but I started to burn out. Now I know routine for business success is less about being available 24/7 and more about taking care of yourself first. I'm all for the hustle life, but it can become toxic if you're not careful. You need balance. My daily routine starts with a great morning, priming (thank you, Tony Robbins), a great breakfast and journaling. Then, when I know I'm feeling great and my mindset is strong, that's when I start my business calls and building activities. At the same time, focusing on myself is the best way to overcome any fear or self-sabotaging thoughts because I'm constantly reminding myself of my goals and my mission. Everything else after that becomes easy.

"We make a living
by what we get,
we make a life
by what we give."

—WINSTON CHURCHILL

CHAPTER 10

ETERNAL MENTORS

Features of Fortune

- Compassion
- Confidence
- Authenticity
- Enthusiasm
- Attentiveness
- Discernment

I've told you a little bit about Alex, who is dearly missed, and this book could not do enough justice describing the man he was. But I have three figures here who also have incredible lives that revolve around mentorship and dream fulfillment. I look up to their blueprints.

A PARTNER TURNED CORPORATE LEADER: SIMON BOWLER, LONDON, UK

Q. When did you join the industry? Why?

A. I joined as a partner with the company in May 1990. I was in my early twenties, with an entrepreneurial spirit and always open for new challenges. Network marketing seemed like the ideal vehicle to reward people and didn't discriminate in any way shape or form. In 1996, I was invited to join the company in a corporate role and my current position is VP Global Partner Relations.

Q. How did you meet John? How has it been working together over the years?

A. I first met John at a partner meeting in 2009 and from the onset, I knew he was going to be an influential leader within our company. John was part of the huge success we had between 2013-2016 when Gen Y and social media came together, and we had a tsunami of growth in the UK, which eventually rippled out to the rest of the Juice Plus+ world. John has always had his feet on the ground, allowing us to develop a really close relationship built on trust and respect.

Q. What can you share about the success you have seen during your years in the corporate field?

A. We've had phenomenal growth over the years as a company. A huge part of this has to be attributed to the change toward social selling and building on a subscription model where we, as a company, do the heavy lifting for a partner like delivering the product directly to the client, collecting the money, paying commissions, self-billing etc. Even though we've just celebrated our fifty-year anniversary, I still feel like we're a start-up company.

Q. What are the keys to your success? Do you have advice for others who need a Plan B in current times?

A. As a fifty-year-old company, we can offer partners a short-, medium- or long- term career path dependent on what they want from their business. Our business is very simple and the first key to success is to become a "product of the product" and a good ambassador for the company. Most of our partners joining our business were initially satisfied clients. I'm proud to say that 90% of our revenue comes from our regular customer base.

Our business is a marathon and not a sprint and whilst we pay thousands of partners a nice supplementary part-time income each month, the big success comes down the line from building a team—that can take years of hard work and dedication.

Q. What behaviors and routines have you adopted to become successful? How do you manage fear and self-doubt?

A. As with all success to any business, discipline, work ethic and having a massive desire for success is paramount if you want results. Continually working on your self-belief is a daily task and I believe never stops until the day you die. For me, studying and reading about successful people gives me huge motivation and top tips that I can apply to my day job.

Q. What is your vision for where the industry is heading in the future?

A. Network marketing is going through a huge change, and I believe the stigma of the 90s will be a thing of the past as millennials and Gen Z embrace the new age of social selling. Our digital ecosystem is changing people's buying habits and ultimately changing the way we do business. I believe we are the new Amazon or Uber of the direct selling industry where we will become the largest provider of part-time earning opportunities.

Today, our industry is a $180.5 billion goliath and encompasses 119 million representatives worldwide. Think about the numbers and people's lives that are being changed in the process.

WORLD WANDERER, MOVER AND SHAKER: SHAY O'BRIEN, GENEVA, SWITZERLAND

Q. Where are you living and working from during the global shutdown? How are things?

A. A little Spanish island called Ibiza. When we knew the lockdown was coming, we jumped on one of the last flights here. Here, we have a bigger property in the country, with acres and animals. We're experiencing month over month growth. Just got the report today. We had an incredible March and April and now May is jumping up again. We have a health-related supplement, so the growth is there. We have a product related to the times and what is happening. I don't think it would be the same with vacuum cleaners!

Q. What does growth look like to you? What numbers do you look for or a particular formula?

A. As a company, we would be a little bit like the stock market. You have a series of bull years. Then a bear year. If you look historically, the bull market when the market is going up will last four, five, six years. Then you'll run into a natural bear market or combination. This may be the best growth year on record. I've been involved for thirty-one years. Last year wasn't the best for us, but this year, we're starting out to be strong. April is a shorter month, but those rules don't apply. Every day is a Monday or Saturday. You don't expect to grow so quickly.

Our goal is to keep adding products and keep people motivated. For culture, retain those who come in and help them achieve their goals. I'm a shareholder. I was a distributor, part of the corporate team, and then a shareholder. We try to create the environment that people want to be a part of. It's natural to want to be a part of a larger group so we have to make it as interesting and exciting. We have much more women in key positions, like 80 percent. When I go to an awards event celebrating top earners around the world, it's all women. John is one of the few men. There is no age barrier. We're an older organization in the States and younger in Europe. I don't know why. In my thirty-one years, looking at who makes it to the top, there is no one type of background. There is one man in the UK making his way up as a future leader and was a carpenter getting tired of working in the cold. He came in part-time and is fulltime now. Now he's starting to earn serious income and he's enjoying it. I had a call with him the other night and he had 170 people on the call, and he has a 6:30 wakeup call with his team. I asked him how the call was, and he had over 100 people on that call. This is important during this lockdown period. Some people are going literally crazy. Mental health challenges will come in different forms.

Q. You're crafting an environment of belonging and empowerment.

A. Those who are worried about possible upcoming recession, we're giving reassurance in some way. Those who have joined during this virus period are living more positively rather than getting sucked into the anxiety and fear.

It might be interesting to know I have been doing lots of calls for the group, up to a few thousand people. I don't normally do this as shareholder. I have been making big income for a while, and I'm in an investment company also investing in startups and others. I've been getting calls of fear by those we're invested in. I made calls forecasting a huge explosive period. When you look at why, oranges, alternative milks and plant-based products are the fastest growing during this time, it's because people want to be healthy. We're a home-based business and didn't change our model toward productivity. I have just spread the word. As an investor, I have more visibility in the companies that are doing well.

Q. What is your earlier story, and how did you get into network marketing?

A. I was 24 years old, full of enthusiasm and energy, and wanted to live life to the fullest. I didn't feel like working for "the man" was where I wanted to go. I wanted independence. I didn't know what that looked like, but I was open. Then a friend called with an amazing business opportunity. I loved the package of all this without really knowing about it. It's one of those situations like when you talk to someone at a bar and don't know them, but you fall deeply in love with them. That's what I felt like for the company. I didn't know the possible pitfalls but started shelving the rest of my life to do this. I did this 24/7 and traveled everywhere. UK,

Ireland, Brussels, lived in Paris for a year, lived in Milan for a year, Monaco, Newport Beach, San Diego, Los Angeles.

Q. Were all these places part of your strategy or where the business was taking you?

A. Also being in my twenties and single! No ties and excitable. I had a decent six-figure salary in the UK, which was a lot of money then. In those days, it was a fortune, so I had money to live in cool locations. I had a penthouse apartment in Brussels and didn't know it was such a cool place. Then my ambition since I was 14 years old was to live in Paris. I had my thirtieth birthday there. Now, I'm married with three kids, so you can't compare the two realities. On my death bed, I will remember that year in Paris, my wedding, the birth of my first child. I had worked 24/7 to sustain the business and got super into fitness, running around the city all night. I never got over the beauty of the place. I was just in love with it. Then Monaco, and then I got invited to do a joint venture with the corporate team to help build the business further. Then on the directing side for seven different countries, you realize the challenges the corporate guys have. We created a big, incredible family and that was our main focus. Then it grew into a bigger entity.

Just in terms of people reading this, it's important that I had success as a distributor, in corporate, and as an investor.

Q. What were the challenges?

A. I joined in 1989 and we introduced the whole foods products in a capsule product in 1994 and struggled to bring this to Europe. I was on the corporate team and that was a tough time. You've got a supplement that is quite expensive, and you have nothing to say this does anything for you. We needed proof. We created a lot of studies of the highest level of credibility now maybe thirty or forty peer-reviewed with the top universities all over the world. We didn't have a reorder program either. I was living in Milan and switched from being one of the boys as a distributor, to suddenly the corporate guy. Like soccer player to manager. You're not the boss but gatekeeper to how the company is doing. You dig deep during challenging times, learn and move on. How I got staying power? Can I keep this going? What am I made of?

I always had good times and would be talking to 1,000 or 2,000 people from on stage, advocating for people to dig deep and be strong. But I had joined during recession when business was booming. I hadn't experienced a tough time until 1996-2001. My right-hand man was Simon Bowler. My dad, Shay Sr. Without Simon, I would not have made it. He has to be mentioned because you need to have your right-hand man next to you. My dad was a rock-like figure. He was also a great mentor to many.

Q. If you were to think about all these incoming people from around the world and we talked a year from now, what characteristics made those who succeeded?

A. I've seen a lot of people come and go. Timing is key. Life can be that way—a great person but a life event takes the focus from someone. Having said that, I've seen desperation drive the inspiration. Having a purpose and a goal. What is your why? This business is not all roses. The why helps you, good or bad days. Being teachable is very important. "I know nothing, tell me everything." Then the big one is doing it. Work habits are No. 1, with the ability to grow and change. The skills are fairly straightforward, but you may have to grow more armor. Rejection is part of the business. Discipline. Someone the other day said, "Motivation is not my success. It's discipline." Some days, I don't feel motivated, but my discipline is the motivation.

CLIMBING AND SOARING: MONA GRON, COPENHAGEN, DENMARK

Q. What is your most recent achievement?

A. Five minutes ago, I got a promotion! It means I grew my network marketing business to a certain level, with more volume of customers. I have a bigger team now.

Q. How long did that take? What is the benchmark?

A. I've worked every day for one and a half years. This is my fifth promotion during that time. It's a good pace. I've seen a lot of businesses grow fast and then disappear overnight because the culture was not built. I have good relationships with other team leaders. It feels good. It's really weird because I've been working for this a long time and then within ten minutes, I have it! I'm going to retire into my business, that is my plan. This is not a job. This is a lifestyle of living my life and building my business at the same time. It's not something I need a break from. I can do it no matter what age I am. I'm planning to build as strong of a business as John has. My plan is to build this business to an extent that I'm financially independent and that I don't have to worry about anything for my kids and family. I'll do it consistently over time.

Q. What is your earlier life and entry into network marketing?

A. I have a financial education, a bachelor's degree in economics from Copenhagen Business School. I have always been driven to make money, but I've always been a person who likes to help other people. I found that in the health care profession, though I wasn't drawn to it. I went to the financial way. Then a couple of different jobs—a salesperson for copying machines for Cannon and I saw how the guys, all men, were selling a lot of machines. I could do the same thing because I'm good at talking to people. I was working at Cannon in a different role and then got the sales job. I was happy for a while, but I couldn't get excited about machines! It was just machines. Then I started in a corporate management role for the network marketing company I'm now a brand partner with. I started in October 2007 at the bottom, but there was a plan for me to be the manager of the Nordic office. I learned everything from the ground up because I like to know what I'm doing. I am always hungry for the details before I talk about it.

Two years in, they made me the regional manager of Norway, Sweden and Finland with a staff of ten employees I was responsible for. I was the youngest on the team. It was challenging but exciting. I learned so much in that job. I worked for eleven years and traveled a lot, had a lot of responsibilities with the franchise partners, saw a lot of changes in the organization. Through the change and insecurities, I had to be the rock for the team. It all went well in the end, but at some point, the travel became too much for raising my boys. Two years ago, between dealing with a divorce and my youngest son, who needed me, the days away just increased dramatically. If I had two weeks at home, that was drastic. I knew I needed a change. When I do something, I go all-in. I knew if I was going for another job, I would end up as a manager again.

I love the product, the atmosphere, the mission, so I didn't want to let go of this. First, I couldn't figure out what to do, and then I went to a Tony Robbins seminar in London two years ago to the date almost. I made a decision during that event that I would quit the managerial position and do it as an independent franchise partner just like the thousands I had coached over the eleven years. I'm high on certainty though; I like to have things in place, but this was a big unknown. I decided on a late Saturday evening, walking back to the hotel, with my boyfriend, and said it aloud! It's scary when you verbalize things. He said, "If there is anyone who can do this, it's you, Mona." He empowered me even more. So, I did!

Part of making the decision for this transition was John. I didn't want any other mentor but him. We live in Copenhagen and were flying back on Monday. My boss was in London at the time. I told him. I needed to be authentic and not sit there and pretend. The great person he is, and this says a lot about the company, was that he was in full support of my transition. For six months, I still worked for the company in a solid transition period. I had an off period, then started up the business with John. He's just always there. He's the most amazing mentor. I don't know how many people he is in contact with, but he has this ability to make sure you feel important, like the only person in the world.

Q. Two years after your big decision night, how would you characterize life as a franchise partner?

A. I've talked to many franchise partners with crazy big businesses. I've seen their good sides and their ugly sides that I dislike. We all have ugly sides, but everything I have seen John do, his partying whenever I've seen it, is as "ugly" as it gets. And that is not even ugly. He's so genuine. He had leaders in the Nordic region, so we've known each other eight years or so. We've been through a lot of dramas and circumstances, but John has always kept calm. I hate drama. I don't mind dealing with issues and situations but gossiping and not looking for solutions—all the bitterness—I have such low tolerance. John knows what he is doing. He and two other people revolutionized the JuicePlus business when they got started in 2011, 2012, with using social media. At the same time, he is very humble and down to earth.

It's worth adding that it just hit me that no one talks about this, but when I worked as a salesperson, for instance, it was a guy's world. The tone was different. The humor could be sexist with undertones, not necessarily sexual all the time, but uncomfortable. With our business, I haven't had this with corporate staff or the majority. No concern of emphasis on you are a man or woman, what color your face is. If he did have this tone of sexuality or sexism, it wouldn't succeed. There are too many people involved. You need to be aware of your communication style and eliminate any signals or wrong innuendos. Managing with complete neutrality or it could be disturbing or hamper people from doing their job. We build people up, their confidence, their skill sets, mindset, health, so it would just be a mess if these things got in the way. I try to be a master of this.

Q. Can you share any goals?

A. This coronavirus crisis has just made a powerful impact on this business. I'm working the same way I used to from home, with my computer, phone, Zoom, the exact way before lockdown. Of course, I met more people in person, but this business is just taking off. Business is exploding, which has helped my separate business. We have a lockdown in Denmark and the US. Some people are getting laid off so it's scary for people. We have a plan B to offer, and it's only $50 to start, so it's absolutely risk-free. You can work from anywhere, but you're not alone because you have mentors like John and me. So, the world's biggest crisis in our lifetime has helped our business explode. Before the crisis, people thought it was a good idea to have a Plan B; now, it's essential. You can't just rely on the main setup you have. In a month, with May going crazy, there is no telling. If you are teachable and hungry, anyone can do this. And now I get to work with my sister. She joined in October and she got a promotion today as well. This business makes a big difference to a lot of people.

"You can motivate by fear, and you can motivate by reward. But both those methods are only temporary. **The only lasting thing is self-motivation."**

—HOMER RICE

CHAPTER 11

REIMAGINING THE FUTURE

Features of Fortune

- Inspiration
- Exuberance
- Worth
- Strength
- Celebration
- Self-awareness

How many times have you reimagined your future? I hope you're at least starting to in the process of reading *Between Fear and Fortune*! I'm all about positive examples, and the following two women epitomize future-forward dream makers in case you want to know how it's done. They are forthright and as genuine as they come.

FIT, HEALTHY, FABULOUS COMPANY:
EMMA SNEDDON, COUNTY DONEGAL, IRELAND

Q. What was your earlier life and how did you get started with network marketing?

A. John and I met in 2012. I was a busy working mom with three children. I just returned to work after a year. I fulfilled high expectations from corporate jobs. I was looking for a fitness program and personal training that would fit my lifestyle and early in the morning. It was my son's nursery nurse. I saw the transformation in her, and she recommended him, like alignment of the stars. I'm all in if I do anything. From May, I went every morning and John and I got on really well. He didn't mention network marketing for a while. In October, he mentioned it, but I wasn't interested at all. I wasn't eating breakfast, running on empty, and then he mentioned the product. John finds common ground in any topic and with anyone. His training wasn't just on the clock—he was committed to helping you get results. I didn't feel like I was being sold anything. I did fall in love with the product. I wasn't looking for a business opportunity, but then the corporate life didn't do it for me anymore. The more you earn, the more your expenses tend to go up.

I wasn't unhappy, but I started to question that little sliver of a question if I was spending enough time with my kids. I made my success bed and I was lying in it! I was in a rat race not a rut. It was frantic. Sleep, gym, work, repeat, slot the kids in whenever I could. Everything around the house and as a family needed to be squeezed into the weekend. And socializing just a little. I used to go for a massage once a month and the woman told me how amped up, I always showed up in the world. That was how I showed up—a little frantic, hectic. Always thinking ahead and not enjoying the moment. I had a nice house, car, kids in the picture but no time-freedom and space in my head, community. John always said if I told you to do five reps, you would do ten. He thought I would apply the same for this business...if I ever joined!

Q. What behaviors and routines are important to you?

A. It depends on your individual background. I had a 6-figure income, my husband has a 6-figure income, but we kept spending it. We kept one holiday. There was never spare cash. When we got married, we had a lot of individual debt. I was looking for spare cash, enough to go on holiday or strictly for Christmas. We were always too extended before we got to December. I had never heard of network marketing. By my second month, I earned 400 pounds and got energized. I didn't think I did that much other than reconnecting with old friends on social media, high school, univ—everyone is on one social platform or another. Conversations were natural. A lot of them were into health and fitness. So, the skepticism you normally have with strangers wasn't a part of the build-up.

By the end of that first 18 months, I had left my fulltime job and retired my husband from his. I paid for our whole life change. I speak to John more than I speak to anybody. We have a friendship as well and that helps to motivate me. As a 36-year-old working mom, I don't think I would have joined as a stranger. He helped me get my body, mind and life right. I totally trusted him. When I joined the business, funny thing is my husband was like, what in the world is going on? You're spending all this time and money on this guy! John and I traveled all over the country, keeping crazy hours in the car. I probably did all my JuicePlus training in his car or my car. I wanted the blessing from my family to do this for twelve months. It was a big ask. I asked him to stay home and take care of the kids while I gave this my all. He and John became good friends. When I sign people up, I tell them if this works, we're going to be in each other's lives forever. We need a good working relationship. It's important to be honest with people. I speak to John four or five times a day. It's not "transactional."

Q. What is your advice to others?

A. Look at what your life will look like if you don't make any changes. For example, I was going for a promotion and ironically, it would have meant being at home more because the customer focus would be where I lived. I ticked all the boxes, hit all the targets. My boss told me to come four hours' drive with no traffic, so I put the kids in bed, drove overnight and stayed in a hotel for two hours before arriving at the meeting, expecting to get the job. They informed me that they recruited someone else for the job and thanked me for my time. What was the point in this? In the professional environment, you can do everything possible and have no control over the outcome. Is this it for me? In traffic, I just halted the car and thought, I will still be on this motorway maybe with a bit more money but... In twenty years, it will still be the same in this model, 56, 66. I didn't like what I saw. If you do that and you love what you see, great. But if you don't like that image, now is the time to start something new or try something. Now I look at that age and it's really fucking exciting! We need to step back and think about all this. With everything going on in the world right now, more people are looking at this.

Addressing a huge auditorium full of moms (and loads of children) in Phoenix, Arizona, I built my business to national marketing director. Talk about the effects of the product it's had on you. No one can argue with your experience. Content on social media has to be educational and motivational.

PLAN A DUE TO COVID-19: BECKY LANE

Q. What is your background, and how did you get introduced to network marketing?

A. I was introduced to the business by my PT at the time and he asked whether I would like to get on a business call with his upline, John. I was way too shy for that and said no! I didn't meet John until an event in my local town, which was in a rundown hotel. How times have changed! I remember John standing up speaking, sharing his story and thought the business model was too good to be true. However, I did think if he can do it, then I can. John has been a shining light for me over my time in the business. He is a true leader and I hope he will be part of my life for many years to come and see how his support has changed my life. He has guided me and has had faith in me even when I haven't had it in myself. Through my tears and squeals of delight, he has been at the end of the phone. A true friend and mentor.

I joined in desperation. I had been working hard, got paid well but needed a break. I was time-poor and wasn't living my best life. I was told that network marketing could be a vehicle to help me achieve my dreams over a five-year career. Could I "risk" taking the leap of faith? Absolutely! To work from your phone and distribute products worldwide whilst getting paid to be the healthiest version of yourself was a no brainier. I needed change and this was it.

Q. What two words do you associate with success?

A. Belief and consistency. Not only do you grow a business, but you grow within yourself. Take time to feed your mind with positivity, affirmations and alike, it will transform the way you live your life. Care for your customers more than you care for yourself because one day those customers might turn into team members who will help you to grow a business bigger than your wildest dreams. This business has always been my Plan B, which recently became my Plan A due to Covid-19. Overnight, I had to stop working (I'm self-employed and work in schools). However, this business tripled in pay-line over the most economically challenging time for our country. I will always be grateful.

Q. What is your advice to others?

A. I've always known that there is more out there, I just didn't know how to get it. I've been self-employed for most of my working life because business excites me! When you don't feel like you're working, then you know you're in the right place. I have an absolute passion for wanting others to succeed. I will be the one talking to team members past midnight if it means they will achieve something, I will be the first one up in the morning if it helps someone to get over the line. I have learnt to get a thick skin, to not care about people's opinions. This takes time but when you have that rhino skin, no one can knock you back. Treat your business like a business and not a hobby. Have your daily tasks, non-negotiables, and add value. Be kind, be an influencer, and be strong, and you will receive so much in return.

MAKING A MOVE: NATALIE YOUNG

Q. What was your career path before network marketing?

A. Before the business, the only jobs I had were in customer service or in a call center. I was working at Manchester Airport for an airline and life wasn't too great. As a family, we were struggling, I was in debt and burying my head in the sand pretending it wasn't getting worse. It got to the point that I knew a change had to be made and I needed to find something. I just did not know what. I did not know what I was getting into when I joined. I stumbled across the opportunity thinking if I could just earn money for food or some petrol in my tank, that would be a bonus. I instantly fell in love. Network marketing was perfect for me. Around my work and family commitments, from my mobile phone, from home. I soon realized it was the best decision I had ever made!

Q. How did you meet John?

A. I met John through the business, as he is one of my uplines. I think the first time I met him was at a convention in Nice three months into my business. I saw him on stage and resonated with him instantly. He seemed chill a lot like me. It's strange because a few years later, we actually realized our paths had crossed years before! We used to go out in the same circle of friends every week in our late teenage years and hang out in the same crowd. The universe works in crazy ways.

Q. What has been your key to success?

A. Self-belief first. My confidence has grown so much during my time in the business. I had joined as a shy, self-conscious person, and have transformed in that way. Also, I had a strong why. I wanted to change my financial situation and get out of debt. I wanted to be able to stop worrying and change my family's life, and this is what has always kept me going. I'm also thick skinned. It doesn't matter what anyone says to me regarding network marketing, I know there's nothing better out there. It creates chance after chance for normal girls like me to change their lives and create a better future for their families. My advice is jump in, this could change your current situation, your whole life if you want it to.

I was stuck seven years ago, low, unhappy, and wondering how I would ever change that, and the universe delivered this opportunity to me, which I grabbed. I'm very self-motivated now. No one will change your life for you, or motivate you every day, Barr yourself. I am big on self-development; I believe life is 90 percent mindset. Positivity is key. Goal-getting. I love goals and something to work towards. I like doing vision boards and making my goals clear.

Q. What is your advice for others?

A. Put people before yourself. Care about people. Help them. Remember what you want to achieve. Look at what you have achieved and what you want to achieve. So many people do not have the courage to make a move. I'm proud of my choice. I'm proud I didn't listen to negative people and I took a chance. While people are still stuck in certain situations and moaning about it, letting life pass them by, don't be one of those people. Make a move and build on that every single day.

LIVING THE AMERICAN DREAM: KATIE RAVEY

Q. How did you get started in network marketing?

A. I met John nine years ago at The Village Hotel in Bury. Apparently, my brother had been training with this new personal trainer that his friend recommended, and I was being dragged to this "health event". My brother had been getting some nutritional support from John, and let's face it; at the time, he needed it. Being a pro hockey player living off take-outs is not a winning formula! I was skeptical though. This dude had been telling my brother to take these supplements and I wanted to know what they were about, putting my big protective pants on. I was expecting this huge, buff body builder with an ego. No. John was just a little taller than me but had the biggest grin you couldn't help but warm to.

He introduced himself and had no ego. He was just really excited to have us there. I still was skeptical. But after a while, my arms uncrossed, I sat up and I began to engage. He was sharing just the concept behind this supplement and also the business. No sales pitch, just real-life facts and truth, which I bought into. I joined. Little did I know it was John's birthday. An amazing friendship started also.

As a sponge, I wanted to be around John more, so I started attending his bootcamp classes and learned a lot just being around him. I remember one time, I was walking in the ally back to the car alongside him, talking business and he got out his key to open his car, which was an Audi TT. I thought, wow, I want one! I was driving a BMW X3 that I couldn't afford to drive. I was so broke; I would just go to work and the bootcamp always on fumes. John just told me if I worked this business and did X,Y, Z, this and this would happen.

Q. What were your goals?

A. It took me a year, but one day, I started to apply all the things he was telling me to do and my life, little by little, bit by bit, started to change. The thing is I gave up on myself hundreds of times. John never gave up on me, believing in me more than I believed in myself. I was 23 years old, and this was the first time I felt like someone believed in me. Do you know the power of that? The strength it gives someone? It's so magical. John, no matter what, has always been there, and he brought with him his beautiful fiancé, Victoria, who I found a soul sister in. Before all this, I was working three jobs: one in the family business as an operations manager for a new company, a waitress and then in TV/modeling. I was so broke, I had to keep finding ways to make the extra income. But I was miserably unfulfilled, and I lacked purpose and passion, and even excitement for life. I was living off £800 a month and just no way out. I didn't have the greatest of grades, so my opportunities were limited. I was so scared for my future and what I was going to do to move out of my parents' house. To be and adult and have the freedom. To drive a car without worrying the fuel cost or maintenance. To be able to go to a store and buy what I want. Go on vacation if I wanted, but it felt like a story from someone else's book, wanting all of that stuff. Felt so mystical.

But now, life is very different. I went from all of that to moving across to America, my dream as a teenager, living in a beautiful house on the ocean, raising a family in sunshine and palm trees with an abundance freedom, but more than ever, passion and purpose.

Q. What is your advice to others for this type of turnaround?

A. Get clear on what you want. The more specific, the better. Find someone who you can be mentored by and lock arms with them, as they will believe in you and push you when you don't have that in you at that time. Be obsessed with finding ways to add value in all you do and who you are. Create experiences for your customers or following. Business is two things: Marketing and Innovation. If you can get good at finding new what's in those two areas, you will win at business. And it never stops because the world is changing so fast, so do well. The behavior and routines I've adopted as a successful entrepreneur is that I have belief in myself and a vision. The good book says without vision, people perish. I had and still have a vision for my life and what I want it to look like, so that drives me every day in how I show up as a mom, wife and business owner. When you can take control of your thoughts, you can take control of your life.

EATING THEIR WORDS: KELLY ANNE FLYNN

Q. What has been the best part of this business?

A. I've met so many inspirational people, including the late Alex Hamer-Webb. He was so important in my journey, along with John. John gave me the ability to help other girls believe in themselves the way he did me. With great work ethic, consistency and if you're teachable, anything is possible. I loved the thought of the freedom of network marketing.

Q. What was your life like before network marketing?

A. I had been down the traditional business route. I had worked every job under the sun, been there down that route, wore the T-shirt. But the fact I could run this part-time from my phone (back then, I had a full-time job) was fascinating for me. I loved being my own boss. I love people, so it was perfect, but my goal back then was to earn an extra income. Alongside what I did, I was struggling with bills. My confidence was on the floor. My health was shit. I had no direction, but I knew I had so much more to give. At one point, I was doing care-work for the elderly and working up to eighty hours a week. I had a nasty break-up, which led to my life literally spiraling out of control. I was on self-destruct mode. John was definitely my savior at that time.

Q. What is the key to your success?

A. Keeping a positive mindset and consistency. When I became more organized and consistent in my business, I became more successful. Consistency is key. You can't go to the top without consistency and self-belief. If you think you can't and if you think you can, you're right either way! Inside this business, I'm more positive, professional, authentic, and real. I have great enthusiasm for this industry. I'm so passionate about helping people, especially women. I just know this is my calling, and I'm excited for the ladies I haven't even met or had the pleasure to lock arms with. This business really does complete me. As Alex said, "The future is so bright, you got to wear sunglasses." Everyone is afraid. Society will do that to you. My family didn't mean it, but at the very beginning, they tried to put me off massively. "Get a real job." "That will never work." They have eaten their words.

Over the years, I've learned to block out the negativity. I've grown because I chose to. I've been surrounded by amazing people and inspired daily. I'm a work-in-progress and I'm loving every minute of it. If someone ever offers you a seat on a rocket ship, jump on and figure it out later. That's what I did, and I've never looked back.

CONCLUSION

AN ENTREPRENEUR'S EVERY BREATH

You are not alone in your struggles, the stresses, and the business treadmill you're stuck on. What five things do you need to be doing every day? What type of person do you want people to know you as? I hope this book has helped you identify a few qualities!

If self-doubt, comfort zones, resistance to execution and tracking, financial upheaval, or distractions in your personal life are keeping you encased in fear (again, of something that has not actually happened), time is not on your side to change your mindset to fortune. Human beings are so powerful in what they can achieve yet so fragile in the continually ticking clock of life. Time does not stop for anything or anyone. Only in the romance novels!

Whether you furiously go after what you want, or simply can't stop thinking about how to help someone else needing a hand, you can easily stop to assess your traits, abilities, and resources for positive change. This step alone can get instilled in your every breath as your system intakes new information and new habits. Your fortune builds. You may not see the gold every day. You may even forget to look. But it's there.

The final key points I ask you to consider, between your fear and your fortune, are: What is your vision for your future and what do you want? What action will you take? Are you willing to keep going for as long as it takes?

EPILOGUE

IT'S ALL WORTH IT

What am I grateful for? What have I achieved so far? Who have I become? I reflected on these questions for this book as an afterthought and would like to share my answers with you.

People usually join this industry out of inspiration or desperation. I look back on my reasons and it was a mixture of both. I wasn't really desperate, but I wasn't fulfilled, or financially stable. I was inspired, as I could see a dream life of working in the sunshine and living my perfect day. When I first hit that goal of the extra 500 per month part-time, it gave me choices. That's all money is to me—fun tokens and choices. Being able to say yes if a close family member needs help. Being able to say yes, I can afford to go, or yes, I have the time to do it. When you hit that first figure per month that takes the pressure off you or it allows you to do something you've always wanted to do, your belief gets bigger and your work ethic increases. That was one of the first moments I realized it was truly possible to change my life through this vehicle.

If you can attract five customers, you can attract fifty. If you can attract five team members, you can attract fifty, and if your focused, you can hit 5,000 per month if you have hit 500. It's just a case of doing more of what you're already doing. Momentum is the magic ingredient to growth and once you get it, you have to keep feeding it.

Making life more comfortable was always a motivating factor me. Living in a tiny house with my partner, Vicky and Rivvan, was something we were grateful for but wanted to improve. The bathroom didn't have a shower, so every day, we had to take a bath, which was too time-consuming when you had to be up at 5:30 a.m. on most mornings. So, my next goal was to get the bathroom renovated with a hot power shower installed. It's funny, but we talk about life-changing things and you would never consider a shower to be life changing, but it was.

As soon as I knew I could succeed in this business, a flick was switched in my mind and I was relentless in pursuit of any goal I had. It was on my vision board and I knew I would be ticking it off soon. I remember that November, I was on track to earn enough money to get it done. I paid the plumber and the job was completed just before Christmas. I can still remember my first shower and the sense of reward I got from the work that had gone into it. It's always more rewarding when you earn it. I'm sure you've noticed a few jobs around the house you would like to have completed. Get them on your vision board and make it happen.

Doing cool stuff with the people you care about is a theme I talk about a lot with this business. But one of my favorite memories was getting a private helicopter from the Nice airport to Monte Carlo. It was even better because I surprised Vicky with the trip. Her face was a picture when someone came to take our bags and she thought we were going to the taxi area. A way to arrive in style.

The Monaco-Nice trip was a great experience for me and our team in many ways. We took about 350 people to that convention and it really was the start of a massive business surge. We showed the company what was possible with a group of dynamic leaders having tons of fun and changing lives of hundreds of people. The amount of promotions we had across the team was record breaking. The leaders who walked the stage were incredible and we all celebrated together as one big team. It was also my first exercise of freedom.

I was due to fly back on the Sunday afternoon, but a few of the team were staying. I remember thinking that I didn't want to leave. It was such a magical place. The guys we were flying back with came to get me, and the minibus was waiting to take us to the airport. I decided to miss the flight and book another one in a few days.

Those extra days were incredible. But the surprising factor was that when news got around that I was staying, this motivated everyone on the team to book extra time in for our next trip. The people who were part of that story went on to build incredible businesses, and I'm sure that moment played a small part in inspiring them to do a bit more.

That really was my first taste of total life freedom. Being in the zone of abundance and being able to say yes if I wanted to. For me, that's the best thing about our business.

As the business continued to grow and the cheques got bigger, it was time to think about moving into another house. The new shower and bathroom were great, but we had just outgrown the place. Out of curiosity we drove up to a place we had looked at two years previously. At the time, the houses hadn't been completed. But the universe has a funny way of keeping things safe for you and believe it or not, the house we wanted back then was for sale. We just knew it was the one, as the views and energy were perfect. We moved into the house six weeks after a tour of America. Now, people say moving is one of the most stressful things in the world, but this was a breeze. Again, I don't know another business where you can head off to America for six weeks and come back to move straight into your new house.

A trip I'm most proud of is going away to Canada with my parents, as it was always on my mum's bucket list to do a trip like that and she planned it meticulously. We stayed in some incredible places with our friends from the business, Mark and Yvonne. We had a few nights in Vancouver, headed over to Victoria and Tofino on Vancouver Island, then closed off the trip with Whistler and Banff. We took helicopter and sea planes, we saw orca, tasted great wine, and went surfing during the sunrise. To see my mum's face continually lit up over the whole trip was magic. One of the most memorable trips ever.

It was worth every meeting I had done, every early start and late finish, every long drive home after an evening in Brighton or Newcastle. It was worth every no and every time someone said it wasn't a good product or business. It was worth all the knock-backs and all those moments when you wonder if you will ever get there. The other great thing was I got to speak at a few events, too. I like to get some business activity in whenever I can even when it's on vacation. I honestly don't see this as work—just an extension of my personality.

I've been able to visit Australia numerous times, and run retreats in Majorca, Marbella and Thailand. I got engaged in New York City and watched the Nicks play basketball on Christmas Day. There are many more trips and things I've accomplished in this business. I could honestly write a book just on those. I said to someone once, people don't do the stuff we've been able to do in ten lifetimes; never mind ten years. I'm very blessed to be able to have lived this stuff. I don't share it to impress you, but to inspire you and show you that those sorts of stories are waiting to be written by you with your family.

The stories I'm just as proud of are the stories of the team. From helping people get out of debt to hearing people buy their first houses. There aren't many opportunities where everyone can win, but this is one of them. I will also say this is one of the only communities where nobody says you can't. Tell them that you're going for the next promotion and they will say, yes you can. Tell them you want to hit it big this time and they will say, I can't wait to see you on stage. It really is about lifting others up and showing people there is enough room at the top for everyone. This business means nothing without the people and being able to make friends for life, which I'm eternally grateful for. I often joke that there is a sofa for me in every country!

After recent events and the crisis that looms, I feel like the world has switched onto our way of thinking and our way of working. People have realized the daily commute isn't necessary, and they have realized that a plan B is great idea. That it's important to look after your health and that having an online business makes sense. As of writing, we have tripled our order compared to this time last year.

I've said this many a time, but our business model was ahead of its time. It has taken a world in lockdown to see it. This doesn't mean it gets any easier, as you still need to have vision, laser focus and consistency to have a breakthrough, but if you just keep working, your breakthrough will come, my friend, and the good times await.

REFERENCES

Interviews

Kelly Ann Flynn. Written response. July 18, 2020.
Mona Gron. Phone interview. April 30, 2020.
Sinaed Kavanagh. Written response. July 18, 2020.
Becky Lane. Written response. July 12, 2020.
Paula McGuire. Phone interview. April 1, 2020.
Shay O'Brien. Phone interview. May 5, 2020.
Carly Peace. Written response. May 18, 2020.
Emma Sneddon. Phone interview. April 1, 2020.
Emma Caren Wilson. Phone interview. April 30, 2020.
Katie Ravey. Written response. July 14, 2020.
Natalie Young. Written response. July 14, 2020.

Publications

Cox, Jeff. "Coronavirus job losses could total 47 million, unemployment rate may hit 32%, Fed estimates." CNBC. March 30, 2020. https://www.cnbc.com/2020/03/30/coronavirus-job-losses-could-total-47-million-unemployment-rate-of-32percent-fed-says.html

De Becker, Gavin. *The Gift of Fear.* New York, New York: Dell Publishing. 1997.

Demers, Jayson. "7 Key Qualities of an Effective Mentor." *Inc.* October 1, 2014. https://www.inc.com/jayson-demers/7-key-qualities-of-an-effective-mentor.html

Depta, Laura. "12 Amazing Recent Sports Stories You Should Know About." *Bleacher Report.* September 21, 2016. https://bleacherreport.com/articles/2664619-12-amazing-recent-sports-stories-you-should-know-about

Donnelly, Darrin. *Victory Favors the Fearless: How to Defeat the 7 Fears That Hold You Back.* Shamrock New Media, Inc. May 11, 2019.

Duncan, Conrad. "Coronavirus: More than 6.5 million jobs to be lost in UK lockdown, study predicts." *The Independent.* April 19, 2020. https://www.independent.co.uk/news/uk/home-news/coronavirus-lockdown-job-losses-unemployment-recession-university-essex-study-a9472966.html

Hardy, Darren. *The Compound Effect.* Vanguard Press; Csm edition. October 2, 2012.

Longman, Jere. "Mia Hamm, Soccer Star, to Retire Tonight." *The New York Times.* December 8, 2004. https://

www.nytimes.com/2004/12/08/sports/soccer/mia-hamm-soccer-star-to-retire-tonight.html

McDavid. "From Zero to Hero." March 27, 2020.https://www.mcdavidusa.com/blogs/posts/zero-hero-10-famous-athletes-made-big

Orman, Suze. https://www.suzeorman.com.

Tait, Amelia. "'They have you in a cultish grip': the women losing thousands to online beauty schemes." *The Guardian*. June 1, 2019. https://www.theguardian.com/fashion/2019/jun/01/online-beauty-schemes-selling-social-media-younique-arbonne

ACKNOWLEDGEMENTS

Firstly, I want to thank Almighty God for blessing me with talents and an opportunity to use them.

I want to thank and recognize everyone I've worked with over the years from my personal trainer days to everyone who has been part of my team, past and present. Without you, this would not be possible.

I am grateful for the leaders that I get the pleasure to work with day in, day out. You inspire me daily to show up and do more. To the JuicePlus company and corporate leadership team, thank you for all your support and hard work over the years.

To my upline and good friend, Rob Molyneux.

To my mentors, Shay Sr. and Alex, who are both looking down with pride at what we are achieving and the lives we are changing.

Thanks to everyone featured in the book: Becky Lane, Katie Ravey, Kelly Ann Flynn, Sinaed Kavanagh, Mona Gron, Natalie Young, Paula McGuire, Shay O'Brien, Carly Peace, Emma Sneddon, and Emma Caren Wilson. I could have added many more people to the success stories section, so stayed tuned for additional editions for that.

Thanks to Candi Cross at You Talk I Write and LeAnna Weller Smith at Weller Smith Design who helped me write and produce the book—thank you both for your patience and support during these crazy times! And thanks to Vision99 for their ongoing support and to Kathy the super PA.

Thanks to Jo Grobbelaar for helping me swim towards structure and detail, even when I wanted to swim away.

To my parents who, although they might not have understood all my decisions at times, the support and unconditional love was always there. To my brother for the supportive yet sometimes annoying pushes in the right direction.

Finally, my fiancée, Vicky, for your belief in me from day one. You met me when I had nothing and was going nowhere but believed in me more than I believed in myself, I will never forget that.

Hopefully, this has inspired you to keep working and dreaming. Stay focused, stay humble and hustle with heart.

NOTES

NOTES

ABOUT THE AUTHOR

John Holowaty has been a budding entrepreneur since his school days, selling clothes in class, setting up a gardening business, graduating from university and becoming a fitness entrepreneur. Then he became a seven-figure earner, applying systems and strategies to achieve his dreams and help others achieve their dreams. He found a product in JuicePlus that he could believe in and a company that he could align himself with. Since, his success has led to appearing on shows and stages with John C. Maxwell, Grant Cardone, and Eric Worre. *Between Fear and Fortune* is John's debut as an author.

For more info, visit
www.johnholowatymentor.com

Printed in Great Britain
by Amazon

80964365R00122